Ready to go!

IDEAS FOR SCIENCE INVESTIGATIONS

AUTHOR
Stuart Ball

DESIGNER
Rachael Hammond

EDITOR
Gina Walker

ILLUSTRATIONS
Paula Martyr

ASSISTANT EDITOR
David Sandford

COVER ARTWORK
Ian Murray

SERIES DESIGNER
Anna Oliwa

Text © 2000 Stuart Ball
© 2000 Scholastic Ltd

Designed using Adobe Pagemaker
Published by Scholastic Ltd, Villiers House, Clarendon
Avenue, Leamington Spa, Warwickshire CV32 5PR

1234567890   0123456789

British Library Cataloguing-in-Publication Data
A catalogue record for this book is available from the
British Library.

ISBN 0-439-01671-1

Contents

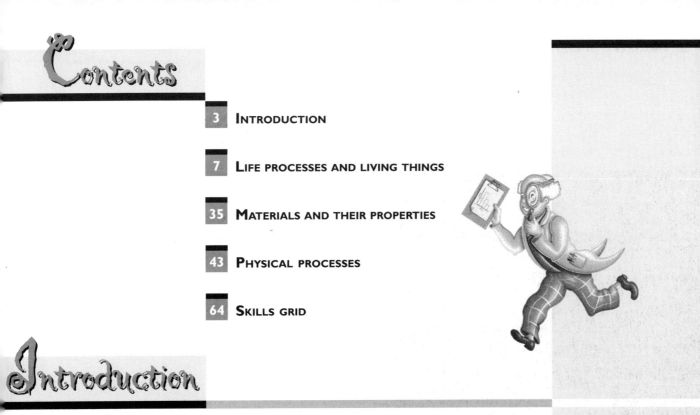

Introduction

Primary science has held its core subject status for over ten years, emphasizing its importance as a vital part of children's education. During this time the skills and processes that scientists use in their everyday lives have found their way into the primary classroom. The evolution of science investigations began in the early days of the National Curriculum, where perhaps it was felt that the skills of investigation would be adequately addressed within coverage of the 15 Attainment Targets. The revision of the curriculum in 1995 reduced the number of Attainment Targets to four, and presented the primary teacher with two programmes of study that provided the basis for scientific investigation: 'Experimental and Investigative Science', or Sc1, and the 'Key Stage Programme of Study', or Sc0.

Children are naturally inquisitive and have an in-built desire to make sense of the world around them. This has been clearly documented by the Nuffield SPACE (Science Processes and Concept Exploration) Project (1990). It shows that children readily create their own perceptions and explanations of the world around them. If we base our science teaching simply on the delivery of facts and knowledge, we develop a science curriculum devoid of rich learning opportunities, as we do not challenge children's preconceptions, which are often misinterpretations. Offering children the opportunity to 'discover' concepts, and thereby challenge their own existing ideas can help to develop more active and receptive learners. Children who are encouraged to question, use their investigative skills and draw upon their existing knowledge to try to explain their observations can develop a self-motivating desire to learn.

So many investigations in the primary classroom, however, are notoriously flawed – too simple or too complicated in their learning outcome. Many teachers feel that children must 'discover' the 'correct' answer. Some may even tell children the outcome – *When you exercise your heart beats faster because...* – and then ask children to carry out an investigation to find this out. Why not just carry out the investigation and let children observe this for themselves?

Using an investigative approach to deliver science concepts and knowledge requires a little more time to organize than the straightforward 'delivery of facts' approach, and teachers need to have a clear understanding of the learning objectives involved. With such an understanding, though, teachers can focus on specific skills for specific children, develop numeracy and literacy skills and develop the use of ICT, all through a well-planned science investigation.

The AKSIS Project (Association for Science Education and Kings College Science Investigation Study 1999) has shown that the fair test type of investigation tends to dominate the investigative activities in the primary classroom. However, there are a variety of investigative approaches to science: *Fair Testing, Classifying and Identifying, Pattern Seeking, Exploring, Investigating Models* and *Making Things*. Using a variety of approaches allows children of all abilities to develop their investigative skills and contribute to their own development in science.

The activities in this book provide the classroom teacher with a means by which to carry out and develop his or her own investigations. They attempt to address the areas teachers may find problematic, such as organization, background science knowledge and how to develop activities that are stimulating yet provide valuable learning experiences. Three photocopiable pages (61, 62 and 63) provide generic templates that can be used to help children plan safe investigations and to record their results on.

ICT IN SCIENCE

Work in science investigations can be enhanced through the use of ICT, but only if the computer is seen as a tool with which children can interact, rather than as a resource to be used in a passive way. Outlined below are some ways in which the various aspects of ICT can be used as part of the science learning in the primary classroom.

WORD PROCESSORS

A word processor can be used to produce a report of a science investigation. But this can be a lengthy process, as children are rarely speedy typists and simply copying up a report is perhaps the ICT equivalent of colouring in! Word-processors in science are best used to produce short direct statements from children about their findings to be printed out or used in a web page or presentation (for instance PowerPoint or Hyperstudio). They are also needed when children are collecting reference materials and cutting and pasting information from a CD-ROM or a website. Word processors are extremely useful when a science report is to be presented in a different way: as a newspaper article, for example. They can also be great motivators, enabling children who have difficulties with writing to express their ideas clearly, by helping them with spelling and presentation.

SPREADSHEETS AND GRAPHING PROGRAMS

Spreadsheets and graphing programs are very similar types of programs, but a spreadsheet offers slightly more flexibility in teaching science, especially in the upper stages of Key Stage 2. A graphing program simply draws graphs: children can enter their results into a table and produce the graph of their choice, depending on the program. Spreadsheets offer more functionality: children can produce graphs and tables, as with a graphing program, but a spreadsheet also allows them to make calculations such as totals and averages automatically. In addition, information can be entered into a spreadsheet to watch a real situation: children can change values and observe the effects on related values. This is called modelling, and can be used to investigate how a child's age or weight might change on a different planet, or the variation of electrical energy consumption in a house.

CD-ROMs IN SCIENCE

Children can use CD-ROMs to research information. Using a CD-ROM to answer questions that they have created themselves offers children a focus to their activity, and using the cut-and-paste facilities, children can select relevant information to use to construct their own reports. Some CD-ROM titles have activities where children can interact and investigate areas such as planetary orbits or the nutritional values of their diets; Microsoft Encarta, for example. Many CD-ROM titles provide animations and video footage, which can be used as demonstrations and can make valuable contributions to children's understanding of science.

DIGITAL CAMERAS

Digital cameras are now readily available at a reasonable price. They enable children to take pictures of their observations to include in their reports. They can also be used to take a sequence of pictures over time – for example, of bread going mouldy – which can be put into a presentation package such as PowerPoint. Here the images can be animated easily to produce a time-lapse effect.

DATA-LOGGING

Measuring is an important feature of science investigations. Data-logging hardware and software allows a range of sensors to be connected to a computer. These can then be used to measure and record temperature, light or sound levels over a period of time. Children are able to see graphs changing in real time. Using sensors gives children a real sense of how important measuring is in science.

THE INTERNET

The Internet gives opportunities to access a seemingly limitless source of information. By 'bookmarking' favourite sites, children can quickly find the information they want: the latest weather reports with satellite images, for example, or up-to-date images from the latest Mars mission. Remember, children need a focus and purpose for their use of the Internet to avoid aimless and time-consuming searching.

The flow of information on the Internet is a two-way process – not only can children access information for researching project, but they can also contribute to the information available for others. They may be able to present their investigation findings on the school website, or exchange details of their scientific data with other schools through e-mail.

ASSESSMENT

Before any of the activities in this book are undertaken it is useful to think about the assessment opportunities they can provide. How they are used, and what they are used to assess very much depends on the learning outcomes that have been decided upon for the lesson. For example, the teacher may wish to assess children on their planning skills. If so, an activity should be chosen that involves fair testing or pattern seeking, and just the parts involving planning and identifying variables should be carried out. If the teacher needs to assess children's ability to analyse data and draw conclusions, then the planning and carrying out of the investigation could be done as a demonstration for the whole class, with children working on an individual basis to analyse the results and record their own ideas.

In assessment, we need to know where children are starting from, so that we know where we want to take them. There are a number of useful strategies that we can employ to highlight children's ideas about scientific concepts. When starting new concepts, the teacher should ask the children to record what they already know. For example, children could be asked to draw what the inside of the body looks like, showing where the organs are and what they are called. After a teaching input, in which these drawings can be used for discussion, children could draw the inside of the body again and make comments about what they have learned.

In investigations, children need to predict and guess outcomes, which provides an ideal opportunity for the teacher to obtain information that can be used for assessment. But to do this effectively, children must be working in an environment that values such an approach and is not overly concerned with obtaining the 'correct' answer. Working in such an environment allows children to feel comfortable about contributing their ideas, makes them more open to other points of view and makes them more receptive to learning.

An extension of such an approach is to use 'concept maps'. Here, children record the words and ideas that they feel are linked to a concept. They then make connections between these words and ideas. The children can be asked to produce maps before and after an investigation or unit of work. These can be compared and differences highlighted, showing how their thinking has changed.

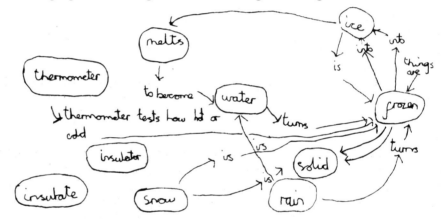

Questioning is an extremely useful tool for assessment, and when it is used to engage children in conversation about their work, deep insights can be made into their scientific thinking.

CROSS-CURRICULAR LINKS

Science investigations also provide useful opportunities to assess other aspects of the curriculum, in particular literacy, numeracy and ICT. By focusing on how children research and present their investigations and write their reports, links can be made to work in literacy. Assessment opportunities for numeracy are provided when children are required to produce graphs, analyse data, use measuring equipment and calculate averages. In ICT we can use spreadsheets, CD-ROMs and data-loggers for assessing ICT, as well as science.

In the activities described in this book, further specific links to other areas of the curriculum can be made through the 'Now or later' sections. For example, there are suggestions of how to extend activities by writing a story, producing a leaflet, going on a visit, taking and manipulating digital photographs, drawing a scale map, designing a survey, and so on – all of which have clear connections with other curriculum subjects.

USEFUL READING
Goldsworthy A and Feasey R, rev. Ball S, *Making Sense of Primary Science Investigations* (1997) ASE.
Sherrington R (ed), *ASE Guide to Primary Science Education* (1998) ASE.

Investigations concerning living things are often difficult to undertake in the primary classroom. This problem can be solved partly, through the use of secondary sources and simulations. Particular attention must be paid to relating these activities to the real world. Allowing children to relate activities to their personal health and to have experience of a variety of environments and habitats will reinforce the learning objectives. Such activities can help children develop a sensitivity to the needs of living things.

BEAT THE CLOCK

RESOURCES AND CLASSROOM ORGANIZATION

Each group will need:
- 'How to measure a pulse' sheet – photocopiable page 22
- two stopwatches/clocks
- 'Pulse recording sheet' – photocopiable page 23
- graph paper
- calculator
- sticky labels to make badges.

If available, a digital pulse meter is particularly useful for children who have difficulty in measuring a pulse.

BACKGROUND KNOWLEDGE

Heart rate increases with exercise. The blood takes important things like oxygen to the muscles; the harder the muscles work, the more oxygen they need each minute, so the faster the heart has to pump to circulate the blood. It is this pumping action of the heart that the children can feel or hear. This is called the pulse.

Children need to know that the heart pumps blood around the body, and be familiar with the names of organs such as the lungs.

WHAT TO DO

Ensure that the children have practised and are able to measure a pulse rate (see photocopiable page 22).

Divide the class into investigation teams. Each team member has a job to do in the team. Use sticky labels to assign jobs to each team member:
- the runner
- the pulse measurers
- the time keepers
- result recorders.

Explain that all team members have very important jobs to do, and that they all rely on each other to produce a good investigation.

Ask the children to make a prediction about how many beats per minute their runner's pulse rate will be at rest, and what the maximum pulse rate will be after the child has been running.

INVESTIGATION TYPE:
EXPLORING

OBJECTIVES
To develop the following skills:
- use of tables and graphs
- taking repeated measurements
- calculating an average
- explaining conclusions in terms of scientific knowledge and understanding.

VOCABULARY
Pulse, pulse rate, heartbeat, blood, artery, vein, oxygen, lungs, muscle.

Decide with the class how far the runners should run. Once this has been decided, follow an investigative procedure similar to that outlined below, using the 'Pulse recording sheet' on page 23:

1 The pulse measurers measure the pulse of the runner at rest, at the wrist and chest – they count the number of heartbeats in 30 seconds, as measured by one of the time keepers.

2 The result recorders multiply the number of heartbeats by two, for both the wrist and chest, and record the two pulse rate measurements in beats per minute.

3 The runner runs for one minute, measured by one of the time keepers. After one minute, the runner stops and sits down.

4 The pulse measurers get to work measuring the runner's pulse again, at the wrist and chest.

5 The result recorders record the two pulse rate measurements in beats per minute.

6 After about a minute, the runner runs again, for a further minute.

7 This process is repeated between eight and ten times.

8 Once completed, the runner sits down and rests. The team measures and records the runner's pulse rate at the wrist and chest, about once every two minutes. This is repeated until the pulse returns near the original resting pulse rate of the runner.

As individuals, or in their teams, the children should then calculate the average pulse rate for each pair of wrist and chest pulse rate measurements. Using this information, they can plot a line graph.

Ask the children to consider their results and compare them to their predictions. They should notice that the runner's pulse rate increases during exercise.

The results should indicate a maximum pulse rate for the runner. So the children should realize that although the pulse rate increases the more active the person is, it is not a continuous pattern. Also, unlike many graphs, this one cannot start at zero (unless the person is dead!)

Discuss with the children the reasons for the increase in pulse rate and how this relates to the function of the heart as a pump.

SAFETY

The activity should take place in a suitable area such as a PE hall, playground or field, where there is enough space for children to run safely. The runners should wear suitable footwear. Be aware of, and sensitive to, the needs of any children with lung or heart problems.

DIFFERENTIATION

Team responsibilities could be allocated according to children's abilities. ICT could be used to produce a graph.

NOW OR LATER

Children could use their observations of how the body behaves while exercising to explain why we sweat, why we breathe faster and how exercise makes us fitter and healthier. They could present ideas as an information leaflet or poster.

BEETLE ALLSORTS

RESOURCES AND CLASSROOM ORGANIZATION

Each group will need:
- a packet of liquorice allsorts
- a 'Liquorice allsort key' sheet – photocopiable page 24
- 'Beetle parts' (sheets 1 & 2) – photocopiable pages 25 and 26
- 'Beetle ID card' sheets – photocopiable page 27
- scissors
- glue.

BACKGROUND KNOWLEDGE

Beetles belong to a group of living things called insects. Insects are non-vertebrates (have no backbone). They have a hard skeleton on the outside called an exoskeleton. Beetles comprise a sub-group of insects called Coleoptera, which includes over 330,000 different types – it is a huge group of animals. There are some really unusual beetles, and some have odd names, such as ladybird, dung beetle and glow-worm.

WHAT TO DO

Ask the class to imagine that the liquorice allsorts are little creatures. You need to identify these 'new' creatures. To do this we use a key.

Explain to the children that scientists cannot possibly remember what every plant and animal looks like. So when they want to identify a living thing that they are not familiar with they use a key.

Divide the class into groups. Give each group a 'Liquorice allsort key' (photocopiable page 24), and a sweet. Ask each group to identify the sweet and report to the class how they identified it.

There may be one or two types of liquorice allsorts that are not identified by the key. The class can discuss how they can make additions to the key to include these unidentified sweets.

Give each group another sweet, and ask them to identify it. They can then record the questions and answers from

the key that led them to this identification, and draw their 'allsorts creature'. They might like to draw eyes, legs and wings on their creature.

With the class, research what type of living thing a beetle is. Give the children copies of the 'Beetle parts' sheets from photocopiable pages 25 and 26. Ask them to design their own beetles, by cutting out the different parts and putting them together in different combinations. Each child should stick his or her beetle onto a 'Beetle ID card' sheet, from photocopiable page 27, and fill in the details. The children need to think about the habitat their beetle might live in, and the colours it might be – they could colour in the creature they have 'discovered'. There is also an opportunity to discuss how living things are given scientific names – and for the children to use the same principles to name their own beetles. All this information can be used to create a computer database.

Once the children have each created a beetle, challenge them to create a key that identifies all the beetles in the class.

OBJECTIVES

To develop the following skills:
- designing and using a simple key
- classifying and identifying living things using keys.

VOCABULARY

Beetle, head, thorax, abdomen, antennae, identify.

SAFETY

Children using scissors should be supervised carefully. The glue used should be a suitable non-toxic adhesive.

DIFFERENTIATION

Some children might find the writing of a key for all the beetles created by the class too difficult, or it might prove too time-consuming. Instead, children could work in groups to produce a key for just those beetles created within their group.

NOW OR LATER

■ Children could devise keys to sort other types of sweets.
■ Children could look for minibeasts or plants in different habitats and use keys to identify the living things that they find.

DESIGN-A-GENES

INVESTIGATION TYPE:
INVESTIGATING MODELS

OBJECTIVES

To develop the following skills:
■ collecting data using secondary sources
■ modelling a real life situation
■ making bar graphs
■ making comparisons between two sets of data.

VOCABULARY

Genes, genetics, DNA, chromosomes, characteristics, inherited.

RESOURCES AND CLASSROOM ORGANIZATION

Each group will need:
■ dice
■ 'Characteristic recording sheet' – photocopiable page 28
■ 'Characteristic cards' (1 and 2) – photocopiable pages 29 and 30.

BACKGROUND KNOWLEDGE

The human body is made up of about 10 trillion cells. Each cell contains a set of instructions that determines not only how we look, but also how to make a human being. The instructions are encoded in a chemical called DNA. This stands for DeoxyriboNucleic Acid. The DNA molecule looks like a spiral staircase – the sequence of steps on the staircase makes up the instructions or genes. The DNA molecules are held in structures called chromosomes.

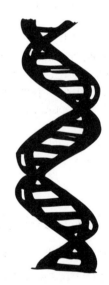

We inherit the set of genes that determines the way we are made from the chromosomes of our biological mother and father.

WHAT TO DO

Before undertaking this activity, be sure that it meets the school's guidelines on sex and health education, or make any necessary changes to ensure that it does so. This activity can be used simply as a data-producing and collecting exercise but it also provides many opportunities to discuss issues such as genetically inherited conditions, and can be used to support a school's sex education policy.

Discuss with the children the following questions:
■ Why do we look like we do?
■ What determines whether each one of us is a boy or a girl?
■ What are genes?

Give a set of 'Characteristic cards', made from photocopiable pages 29 and 30, to each group. The children each have a turn to work through the cards in sequence, throwing a dice for each card to determine the features of a new baby.

Before they roll the dice, ask the children to predict what characteristic will be selected. The probability of a characteristic occurring depends on the card. The children should observe that, for example, there is a greater chance of the new baby being right handed than left handed, or that there is an even chance of it being a boy or a girl.

Once the dice has been rolled, the number shown determines which characteristic from the card the new baby will have. Each child records the chosen characteristics on a 'Characteristic recording sheet' from photocopiable page 28. Once all the cards have been used, each child could design a birth certificate for the new baby.

The children then record their own characteristics and compare them with the new 'person'. Once the whole class has completed the activity, ask the children to undertake a survey of the class about a characteristic of their choice, such as hair colour, or colour of eyes. They need to collect data about themselves *and* the new 'people'.

Once the data has been collected, brainstorm a list of questions with the class that the data could be used to solve; for example, 'What is the most common eye colour?', 'Are there more boys than girls?'

To help answer these questions, children need to produce bar graphs of the data.

This modelling activity helps children to think about how genes are inherited. Of course, this model is random, whereas in real life the genes inherited are determined by the genetic make-up of the parents and previous generations.

DIFFERENTIATION

Some children may find it difficult to survey a whole class and produce a bar graph. Assign children in this position a small group to work with, and ICT to produce a graph. They could also be given a list of questions to answer using their graphs.

NOW OR LATER

■ Once this activity has been completed, there is an opportunity to discuss issues surrounding DNA and genes, such as genetic engineering and genetically modified foods. Many supermarkets have information leaflets about genetically modified foods. Children could be asked to research and produce 'for and against' arguments on such issues.

■ Children could take portrait photos of one another using a digital camera. By using an image manipulation program, they could alter their own facial characteristics.

ROTTEN TOWERS

RESOURCES AND CLASSROOM ORGANIZATION

Each group will need:
■ four two-litre plastic pop bottles (labels removed)
■ plastic insulating tape
■ some old tights
■ 'Make a decomposer tower' instruction sheets – photocopiable page 31
■ 'Keeping it safe!' sheets – photocopiable page 63
■ scissors.

BACKGROUND KNOWLEDGE

Micro-organisms, or microbes, are living things that are so tiny you need a microscope to observe them. They include viruses, bacteria, Protozoa (single-celled organisms) and some algae and fungi. Many microbes are harmful, but some are useful to humans and are used in the manufacture of some foods; for example, yoghurt, beer and cheese.

Penicillin is a drug made from a microbe called *Penicillium*, which is a type of fungus. It is used to kill other micro-organisms – bacteria – when they cause infections in the body.

INVESTIGATION TYPES:
EXPLORING AND MAKING THINGS

OBJECTIVES

To develop the following skills:
■ making careful observations and measurements over a long period of time
■ using the results of observations to draw conclusions
■ using scientific knowledge and understanding to explain conclusions.

VOCABULARY

Micro-organism, microbe, fungi, bacteria, virus, decompose.

WHAT TO DO

Discuss the following questions with children in groups or as a class.

■ What happens to all the waste we produce?
■ What happens to all the leaves that fall from the trees every autumn?
■ What happens to the bodies of dead things?
■ Why does bread go mouldy?

During the discussion highlight words such as 'micro-organism', 'microbe', 'fungi', 'bacteria', 'virus', 'decompose'. Ask the children for their own definitions of these words.

Ask the children to draw what they think a micro-organism looks like. Then use reference sources and ask children to compare their drawings with photographs of real micro-organisms taken using microscopes.

Explain or ask the children to research the roles of micro-organisms. They should realize that micro-organisms are living things, which have an important role in the natural ecosystem, and that some are used by humans in the production of foods. They should also realize, though, that micro-organisms are responsible for illness and disease.

Divide the class into groups. Ask each group to make a tower, using photocopiable page 31. They should then collect some scraps from their lunch boxes, including wrappers, as well as items such as grass and leaves. The children should break all the materials into small pieces, place them in the tower, and spray lightly with water. Finally, the tower should be sealed and placed in a warm place where it can be observed. (The children should ensure that the tower does not dry out by spraying frequently through the meshed air vents on the sides. The tower will also need to be shaken gently from time to time.)

At this point, the children need to record their initial observations and predictions. Ask them to record what they think will happen to the different items in the tower. How long will any changes take?

The investigation may take a few months to complete. Ask the children to record the changes that take place in diaries, either as they themselves notice any changes or as changes are pointed out to them. The liquid that appears at the bottom can be used as liquid fertilizer and the solid matter as compost. Ask the children what they think these 'new' substances are. Explain to the children how in the environment this process recycles materials that have been produced by living things. They should also notice that plastic wrappers have not decomposed. Ask them what consequences they think this might have for the environment.

SAFETY

Ask the children to complete the 'Keeping it safe!' sheet (photocopiable page 63), and to carry out their own risk assessment. It is always important to apply safe and hygienic techniques when dealing with micro-organisms of any type.

Once the towers have been sealed, *do not open them*. When the investigation is completed, wrap the towers in a polythene bag and dispose of them in a dustbin. Whenever children handle them, make sure they wash their hands straight afterwards with soap and warm water. Teach the children never to put anything into their mouths when they are working with micro-organisms.

DIFFERENTIATION

Children could record the changes in the towers through the use of drawings. These could be discussed with each child to determine his or her level of understanding.

NOW OR LATER

■ Organize a 'microbe lunch'. Children could make their own bread and ginger beer using yeast. They could buy or grow their own mushrooms and make soup (or buy the tinned stuff!), and buy or make their own yoghurt. The children could produce a menu for the lunch, which describes the micro-organisms used to produce each food.

■ In contrast, children could research harmful micro-organisms such as viruses and those bacteria that cause food poisoning. They could make and design leaflets and posters that promote good hygiene.

■ Children could write an imaginative story that describes the life of a microbe living at 'Rotten Towers'.

DO PLANTS LIKE LEMONADE?

RESOURCES AND CLASSROOM ORGANIZATION

Each group will need:
■ egg boxes or film canisters
■ cotton wool
■ seeds (e.g. cress, grass or mustard)
■ measuring cylinder or jug
■ various liquids e.g. milk, lemonade, shampoo, vinegar, squash, cold tea, salty water.

Growing times for seeds vary. It is advisable to plan ahead and grow some of the seeds you will be using, to determine how long they take to reach a usable size.

BACKGROUND KNOWLEDGE

Green plants use water during photosynthesis, to produce sugar (food). The other substance required for this process, which is driven by energy from sunlight, is carbon dioxide from the air. Plants also use water for support – when their cells are full of water, they are rigid and can help to hold the plant upright. When a plant does not have enough water, it wilts.

INVESTIGATION TYPE:
FAIR TESTING

OBJECTIVES
To develop the following skills:
■ using apparatus and equipment
■ making careful observations and judgements
■ planning a simple fair test.

VOCABULARY
Germinate, growth, conditions, compost, stem, root, leaf, seed, seedling.

Plants take in water through their roots. The water is absorbed into a plant's root system as it is lost through the leaves. This is called transpiration. Plants do *not* 'suck up' water.

WHAT TO DO

Find out the children's ideas about plants and water. Discuss with them the following questions.

■ Can we give plants liquids other than water?

■ What sorts of liquids should we try?

■ What might happen to the plants?

■ How much liquid should we give the plants?

Plant the seeds in egg box sections or film canisters, on damp cotton wool, and allow them to germinate and grow to a point where they are easy to observe. Once the children have decided on what liquids and how much to use then they can start the investigation.

Assign different pots to be 'watered' using different liquids. 'Water' every day with the chosen liquids. Include one plant that will be given ordinary water; this can be used as a 'control'. The children can then compare all their results with this and make comparisons, finding out if the alternative liquids are better or worse for the plant's development. Ask the children to observe the effects and count the days the plants survive. They can also note any other changes in each plant's appearance. Continue the investigation until there is no further change in the plants. Children can record the results in a table and plot a bar graph showing the effects of 'watering' the plant with different liquids.

Ask the children to compare the final results with their predictions. Were there any unexpected results? Ensure that the children record the conclusions they reached, based on the results – what do they think are the reasons for the results? Were there any other liquids that gave the same results as water? Those plants receiving liquids that are composed mainly of water will probably not die – indeed, lemonade is surprisingly good for plants. Others liquids such as vinegar and washing up liquid will poison the plants.

SAFETY

Children must wash their hands after they handle soils. Any soil samples taken from gardens must be treated carefully as they may be contaminated.

DIFFERENTIATION

Children could record the results pictorially in the form of a simple diary, if they are not able to record the results in a table.

More able children could design an investigation into the effects on a plant of changing other variables, such as the amount or colour of light it receives, the volume of water provided and the surrounding temperature.

NOW OR LATER

■ Children could investigate plants and water further. By depriving plants of water until they wilt, they could observe how quickly they respond when watered.

■ By using a stemmed flower or celery placed in coloured water, children can observe the way water is transported through the plant.

■ Children could look at the way plants like cacti are adapted to conserve water.

BRUSHING YOUR TEETH

RESOURCES AND CLASSROOM ORGANIZATION
Each group will need:
■ toothbrushes
■ ceramic tile
■ various tubes of toothpaste
■ insulating tape
■ solid dark shoe polish
■ stopwatch/clock
■ 'Brushing your teeth' recording sheets – photocopiable page 32
■ 'Investigation planning sheet' - photocopiable page 61.

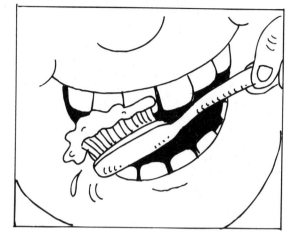

OBJECTIVES
To develop the following skills:
■ using apparatus and equipment
■ making careful observations and judgements
■ planning a simple fair test.

VOCABULARY
Fluoride, decay, cavity, enamel, plaque.

BACKGROUND KNOWLEDGE
Teeth are covered with a hard, strong outer layer called enamel. Bacteria turn food that is stuck to the teeth into acid, which causes tooth decay. The bacteria form a layer called plaque. Brushing removes this layer, and the stuck food. Fluoride is a chemical that is added to toothpaste, which helps to protect teeth against decay.

WHAT TO DO
Divide a ceramic tile into four sections and cover the edges using the insulating tape. On the *unglazed* side, coat each section with a thin layer of shoe polish and allow it to dry. (Make as many of these test tiles as needed.)

Ask the children to think about what is involved when they brush their teeth:
■ the toothpaste
■ the length of time they brush
■ the type of toothbrush
■ the way they brush.

These are the things they could change in order to investigate tooth-brushing – they are called 'variables'.

The children need to construct a question; for example, 'Which toothpaste will clean the best?' or 'What will happen if I brush for a longer time?' Then they must decide what to change in order to answer their question.

To find out the effect of changing one of these variables, the children need to observe the differences in the shoe polish samples after brushing. These differences cannot easily be measured, so the children must make comparisons between each

sample, which can be drawn on the 'Brushing your teeth' recording sheet (photocopiable page 32).

Discuss with the children how they can make their test fair. This involves keeping unchanged all the variables except the one they have selected for investigation.

The children can record all their ideas and comparisons on the recording sheet.

The recording sheet shows a square, which represents the tile divided into the four test areas. The children must decide what titles to put in for each test area, and can make drawings to show their results.

Once the investigation is completed, the children can record their conclusions on the recording sheet.

SAFETY

Putting tape on the tile not only covers any sharp edges, but also prevents it from shattering if it is dropped accidentally. (Put a cross of tape on the glazed side for extra safety.)

DIFFERENTIATION

Children who are not able to construct their own question for investigation could be given a question, and advised what variable they should change and what things they must keep the same.

NOW OR LATER

■ Children could design a poster or leaflet promoting good dental hygiene.
■ Children could invent their own toothpaste and produce an advert to promote it.

WHEN I GROW UP I WANT TO BE A HEALTHY PLANT!

INVESTIGATION TYPE:
FAIR TESTING

OBJECTIVES
To develop the following skills:
■ using apparatus and equipment
■ making careful observations and judgements
■ planning a simple investigation.

VOCABULARY
Germinate, growth, conditions, compost, soil, stem, root, leaf, seed, seedling.

RESOURCES AND CLASSROOM ORGANIZATION

Each group will need:
■ small plant pots or similar containers e.g. cut-down pop bottles
■ seeds (large seeds e.g. broad bean or sunflower)
■ 'Data recording sheet' – photocopiable page 62
■ various soil substitutes e.g. soil, potting compost, sand, stones/ gravel; also more unusual suggestions e.g. paper tissue, flour, used tea bags.

BACKGROUND KNOWLEDGE

The seeds should all germinate, as the seed provides a reserve of food and nutrients. Once the plant exhausts this reserve and begins to require nutrients from the soil, which it obtains through

its roots, then growth will be affected by the type of soil surrounding the roots. For plants to grow well, they need a nutrient-rich environment that allows the roots and shoots to develop. Potting compost is ideal for this.

It is important to emphasize to the children that *nutrients are not the same as food*. Plants make their own food using sunlight. Plants need nutrients from the soil to use in the biochemical processes involved in growth. If plants did actually eat soil as food, then the soil in plant pots would quickly disappear. (Ask the children to imagine, if plants did eat soil, how much a large tree would eat! How much would a whole woodland get through?!) The nutrients in the soil are replaced as organic matter decomposes (see 'Rotten Towers', page 11).

WHAT TO DO

Find out the children's ideas about plants and soil. Discuss with them the following questions.
- What do plants need to grow well?
- What might happen to plants when we grow them in different 'soils'?
- What sorts of 'soils' should we try?
- How will we make this investigation fair?
- How will we measure the results?

Divide the class into small groups. To each group allocate one 'soil' to work with. Each group plants their seed at the same time, using the same amount of 'soil' and the same sized pots. Make sure that each group plants the seed at approximately the same depth in the soil. As a class, decide when to water the plants, and how much water to give (about 5ml each day). Place all the pots in the same area, which should be warm and well lit. At this point, identify to the class that they have only changed the type of soil from pot to pot; everything else – the light, temperature and water – are kept the same. This will make the investigation fair.

Discuss with the children how they are going to measure the effect of changing the soil. They could do this by measuring the increase in height of the plant every day, from the time it first appears above the soil. They could also make predictions about each other's plants and think how they might develop. Each group could record their results on the 'Data recording sheet' (photocopiable page 62), and plot a graph to show the plant's growth over time.

Once the investigation is completed, ask each group to present a report to the class. They could discuss their predictions, show their recording, and talk about the reasons for the results they got.

SAFETY

Children must wash their hands after they handle soils. Any soil samples taken from gardens must be treated carefully as they may be contaminated.

DIFFERENTIATION

Children could record the results of plant growth by cutting out lengths of paper that match the height of the plant. These could be stuck in order on paper to make a graph of growth against time. Children could then be asked to compare the growth with that of other groups' plants, and say if their own plant grew well or not.

NOW OR LATER

- Children could collect soil samples from each other's gardens and see in which one plants grow best.
- Children could have a competition to see who can grow the tallest sunflower. They could find out how they can improve the conditions to maximize plant growth; for example, by using a greenhouse or adding extra nutrients to the soil.
- Using a digital camera, the children could take pictures of the plants as the investigation progresses. A centimetre ruler could be placed next to the plant for comparison. These images can be put in sequence into a multimedia package such as PowerPoint and animated to give a time-lapse effect.

WHERE WOULD YOU FIND THE MOST DAISIES?

OBJECTIVES

To develop the following skills:
■ devising questions to investigate
■ collecting and sampling data
■ identifying patterns in results
■ using scientific knowledge and understanding to offer explanations for any observable patterns.

VOCABULARY

Sampling, quadrat, distribution, pattern, flower, stem, leaves.

RESOURCES AND CLASSROOM ORGANIZATION

Each group will need:
■ measuring tape
■ quadrat or frisbee
■ light meter
■ 'Sampling game rules' sheets – photocopiable page 33
■ 'Sampling game cards' – photocopiable page 34
■ 'Investigation planning sheet' - photocopiable page 61
■ 'Data recording sheet' – photocopiable page 62
■ graph paper.

BACKGROUND KNOWLEDGE

Plants have been chosen to illustrate this example, but these techniques can be applied to looking for minibeasts. Plants are easier to find and count. Ideal species include daises, plantain, dandelion and clover.

When measuring the lengths of stems, ask the children to carefully feel down to the base of the stem and measure from there.

WHAT TO DO

In this activity, children plan and carry out an investigation to see how environmental factors affect the way certain plants grow in an area.

Ask the children to remind themselves about the things plants need to grow. Ask them whether they think there might be any difference in the same kinds of plants growing in different areas. Because the plants are in different areas, are they getting the same amount of light? Would there be more plants in a shaded area or a well-lit area? Are daisies taller in long grass than in short grass? Are there more daisies at the top of a slope than at the bottom? These questions could be investigated.

Children should be encouraged to offer answers to their questions, and give reasons for their answers based on their current knowledge and understanding. These can be recorded and used later for assessment purposes.

Once the children have decided on a question that they would like to investigate, ask them to plan their investigation – they could use the 'Investigation planning sheet' (photocopiable page 61) to help them. At this point you need to discuss with the class the difficulties in planning this type of investigation and how it differs from a 'fair test'.

Point out to the children that it would be almost impossible to count or measure *all* the plants in a large area so we need to use a technique called sampling, where small parts are chosen, and the plants counted or measured in those sample areas. But how do we choose the sample areas? We need to make sure that we haven't chosen areas that just happen to have lots of plants in, for example. We need to use a method that *randomly* selects *lots* of sample areas so that we obtain a more accurate representation of the plants over the wider surroundings.

To give the children an idea of why we need to sample, make and play the sampling game, using photocopiable pages 33 and 34.

Find a part of the school grounds or a place visited that has some environmental difference; for example, light and shade, high and low (such as at the top and bottom of a slope), or long and short grass.

Ask the children to throw the quadrat or frisbee in the chosen area. They need to do this with their eyes closed, and also change direction each time they throw, to try to make the selection of sample areas a more random process. The children need to take lots of samples, as this will provide more accurate results.

Where the quadrat lands, ask the children to count or measure the plants under it (whatever plant the children have chosen to study).

If the children are investigating the effect of light levels on plant distribution, they should count the number of plants and also measure the light level at each sample point, using a light meter. This process should then be repeated at 5–10 different sample points across shady and light areas. Alternatively, a line could be marked out from the shady area to the light area and samples taken at every metre.

The children need to record their results on a table (see the 'Data recording sheet', photocopiable page 62) and use this to make a graph. This could be a bar graph comparing each area or a scatter graph.

Ask the children to analyse their results to see if they can identify a pattern, and suggest reasons for their pattern. If there is no obvious pattern to identify, the children can still make valid comments such as 'These plants are not affected by changes in light'. They can consider how the results compare to their original ideas. How have the results changed their thinking? They may also consider the effectiveness of their sampling and how they could improve their investigation.

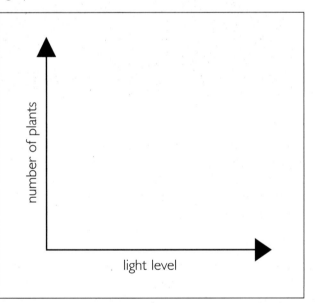

SAFETY

Children need to be aware of the consequences of picking plants and the damage it can cause to some species. They also need to be aware of plants that are poisonous or can sting.

Great care must be taken when children are throwing the quadrats or frisbees, to avoid injury of others.

DIFFERENTIATION

Some children may find it difficult to sample. As an alternative, they could see how many daisies (or other plants) they can count in an area in a fixed time period, such as ten seconds. By doing this in two contrasting areas, children can have the opportunity to try to identify any pattern.

More able children could be encouraged to think about more complicated investigations that could take place over a larger number of areas and longer periods of time. For example, they could plan an investigation to see if the number of different plant species in an area changes over a year and whether this is affected by the seasons.

NOW OR LATER

The class could carry out a survey of the school grounds. Recording the most and least common plants and where they can be found. This could be recorded on a plan of the school grounds.

KNEE BONE IS CONNECTED TO THE LEG BONE!

INVESTIGATION TYPE:
PATTERN SEEKING

OBJECTIVES

To develop the following skills:
■ devising questions to investigate
■ collecting and organizing data
■ examining different graph formats
■ using measuring equipment
■ identifying patterns in results
■ using scientific knowledge and understanding to offer explanations for any observable patterns.

VOCABULARY

Bones, skeleton, joint, measure, growth, age, scatter graph.

RESOURCES AND CLASSROOM ORGANIZATION

Each group will need:
■ measuring equipment e.g. rulers, callipers, measuring tape

BACKGROUND KNOWLEDGE

Children often think that we continue to grow as we get older. It is not always obvious to them that, if this were the case, people who are in their eighties would be very tall indeed! But to children, people who are older are often taller than themselves, so this belief is based on their own observations. Humans grow rapidly in their early years, but this rate gradually slows and stops at around 20 years of age.

WHAT TO DO

Discuss with the children their ideas about 'getting older' and what changes take place as we get older. For example, we get taller, our feet get bigger, we learn more, and so on.

Explain that you have noticed that children in the older classes are generally taller than themselves, and that children in the younger classes are often shorter than them. How could they collect some evidence to investigate the question 'Do we get taller as we get older?' Suggest to them that one way of measuring a person, rather than measuring the total height, is to measure the length of one bone. This can then be compared with similar measurements in other people.

Discuss with the children how they could gather enough evidence to try to answer the question 'Do we get taller as we get older?' The children must decide on the age range that they need to cover and the bone in the body they are going to measure. The bone chosen doesn't really matter and could be left to individual children or groups. It is much easier to measure a bone from joint to joint; for example, from wrist to elbow or knee to ankle.

As the children will be measuring different ages it would be difficult to plot a bar graph for each individual age. The children could be introduced to scatter graphs – using this method of presenting data, children can develop an understanding that there is no need to take a measurement for every single age in the age range that they have chosen. So the children must decide how many measurements they should take. Who are they going to measure? Are there enough people in school to get enough evidence or will they have to do some research at home? Once the children have made these decisions they can begin to carry out the investigation.

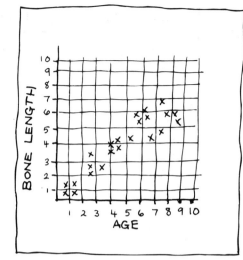

Typically, the children need to measure at least 20 people from a wide range of ages, but the more measurements they take the better the pattern on the graph. The children need to organize their data in a table, recording each person's age and length of bone in centimetres.

Each data point can then be plotted on graph axes showing bone length on the vertical axis and age along the horizontal axis. The children should plot each point where vertical and horizontal lines extending from the age and bone length values would meet. They need to be shown how to read such a graph; they should be able to observe that as age increases the pattern of points gradually moves up, but after a certain age the line levels off. The children could draw a line of 'best fit' that passes through most of the points. (The line should *not* join all the points up, but simply illustrate the general pattern.)

Ask the children to analyse their data and record their conclusions. They should be able to interpret their graphs to see that people grow quite quickly when they are young, but that as they get older the rate of growth gradually slows and stops. Ask the children to make a statement to describe this, such as 'Your bones grow very quickly when you are young, and then stop growing'.

Analysis of the children's graphs can lead to discussion about why eating a balanced diet is important when you are young, and how older people's bodies, although they have stopped growing, still need all the elements of a balanced diet as they are continually maintaining and repairing themselves.

DIFFERENTIATION

More able children could investigate their own questions; for example, 'Do taller people have longer legs?', 'Do you get heavier as you get older?', 'Do people who have big hands have big feet?' They could also calculate the average height, or weight, or length of arm for people at different ages and plot a graph to show how this develops.

Less able children might have difficulty constructing and interpreting a scatter graph. Instead, they could make representations of their measurements by drawing the lengths on paper and cutting them out; by putting them in order of age, the children will have a visual record of their results that they can interpret. It might also help if the children were asked to measure fewer people, and were able to record the sizes of hands or feet by drawing around them.

NOW OR LATER

■ Children could use secondary sources, such as information leaflets about health and food, to find out about nutrition and the food required for a healthy diet. They could produce their own healthy eating promotion posters and leaflets.

■ Children could research what foods are needed to develop a strong and healthy skeleton. What is it in these foods that our bones need to grow and develop?

■ Children could undertake a joke study. They could start with the question 'Do people with the longest funny bones tell the best jokes?' They could measure the length of people's upper arm bone, which is called the humerus, and then ask them to tell a joke. The children could mark the jokes out of ten for how funny they are. They can discuss the scientific validity of this investigation, and make a collection of the jokes people tell.

How to measure a pulse

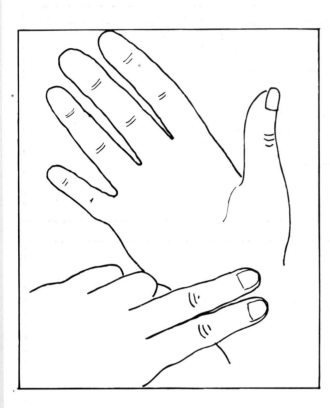

■ Find your pulse on your right wrist, just under your thumb.
■ Lightly press this area with two fingers to measure your pulse rate.
■ Count the number of heartbeats in 30 seconds. Then multiply the answer by two.
■ This gives you the pulse rate in **b**eats **p**er **m**inute (bpm).

Make a pulse meter

Make this simple pulse meter, using a small piece of Plasticine and a plastic straw. To measure the pulse, count the number of times it wobbles in 30 seconds.

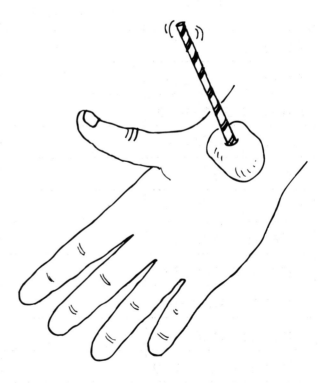

Photocopiables

Pulse recording sheet

The units I am using to measure pulse are:

Equipment list:

	My prediction	Actual result
Pulse at rest		
Maximum pulse rate		

These are the reasons for my prediction:

Time intervals	Chest pulse rate	Wrist pulse rate	Average pulse rate
At rest			
After 1st minute			
After 2nd minute			
After 3rd minute			
After 4th minute			
After 5th minute			
After 6th minute			
After 7th minute			
After 8th minute			
After 9th minute			
After 10th minute			

Liquorice allsort key

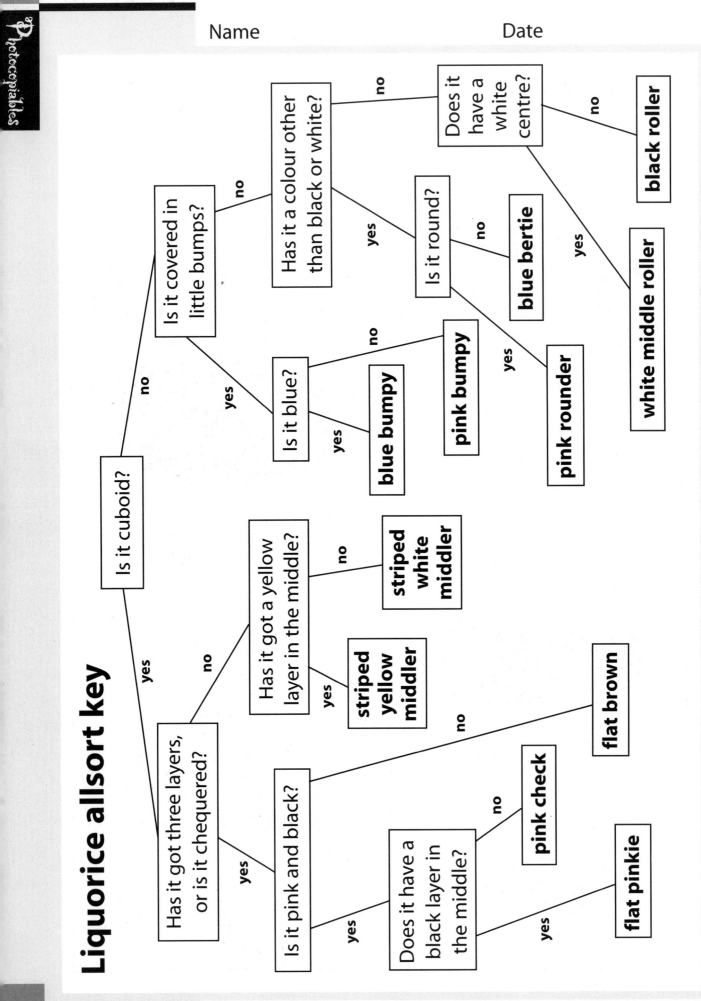

Beetle parts 1

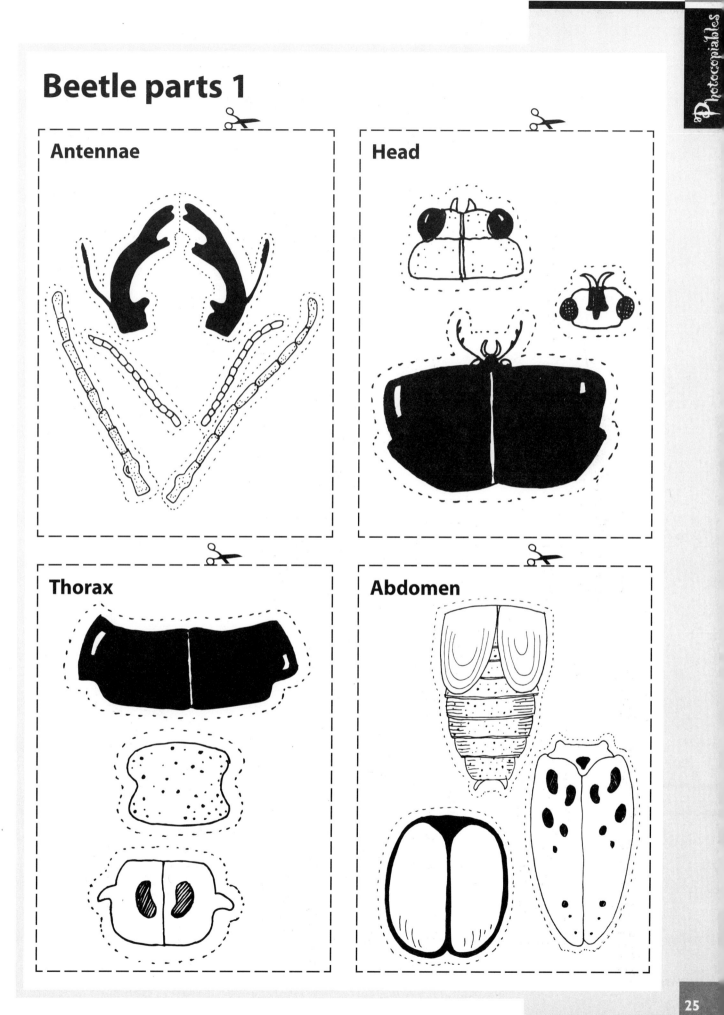

Antennae

Head

Thorax

Abdomen

Ready to go! IDEAS FOR SCIENCE INVESTIGATIONS

Beetle parts 2

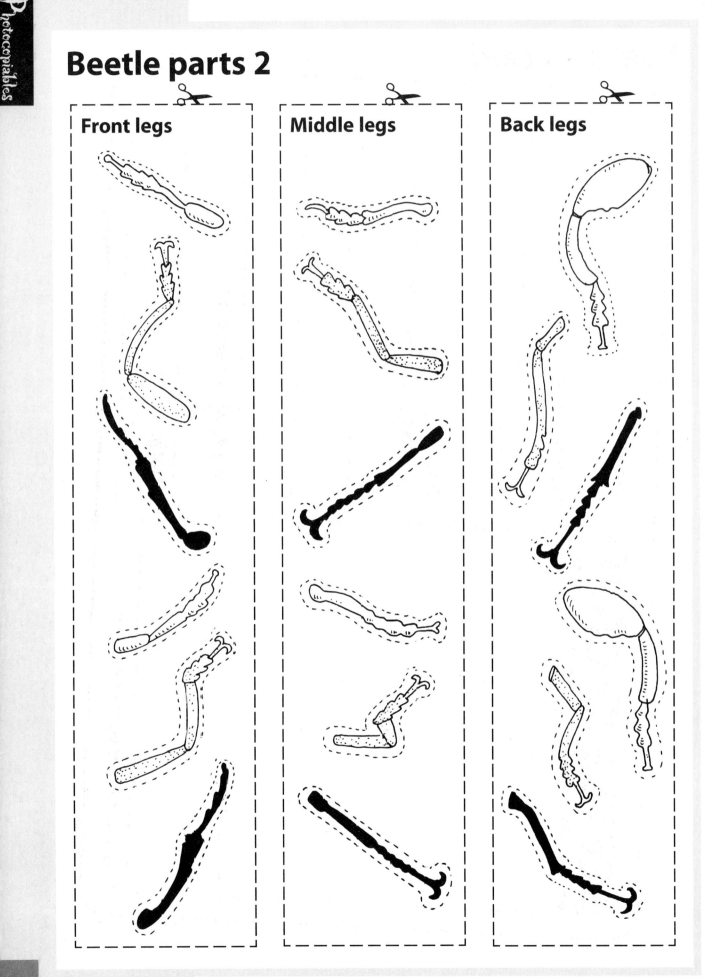

Front legs

Middle legs

Back legs

Beetle ID card

BEETLE ID CARD

Name: _____

Scientific name: _____

Habitat: _____

Notes:
(how it lives, what it eats and so on)

_____

_____

Beetle discovered by: _____

Date: _____

Add a picture of your beetle here

Characteristic recording sheet

Roll the dice and record the characteristic chosen from the Characteristic cards.
Compare these with your own characteristics.

Characteristic	Your new person's characteristics	Your own characteristics
Boy or girl?		
Colour of eyes?		
Colour of hair?		
Left or right handed?		
Height?		
Type of hair?		
Wears glasses?		
Can roll tongue?		

Draw a picture of your new person. Try to include as many of the characteristics as you can.

Characteristic cards 1

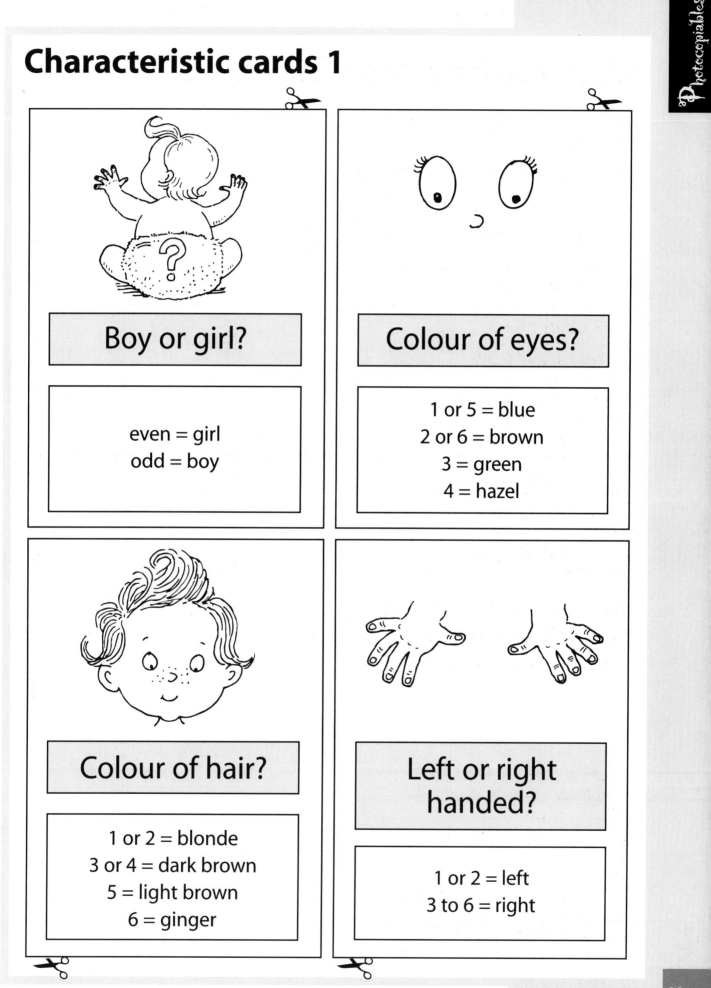

Boy or girl?

even = girl
odd = boy

Colour of eyes?

1 or 5 = blue
2 or 6 = brown
3 = green
4 = hazel

Colour of hair?

1 or 2 = blonde
3 or 4 = dark brown
5 = light brown
6 = ginger

Left or right handed?

1 or 2 = left
3 to 6 = right

Characteristic cards 2

Height?

1 or 2 = tall
3 or 4 = medium
5 or 6 = short

Type of hair?

1 or 2 = straight
3 or 4 = wavy
5 or 6 = curly

Wears glasses?

1 to 5 = does not wear glasses
6 = wears glasses

Can roll tongue?

1 to 4 = can roll tongue
5 or 6 = cannot roll tongue

Name   Date

Make a decomposer tower

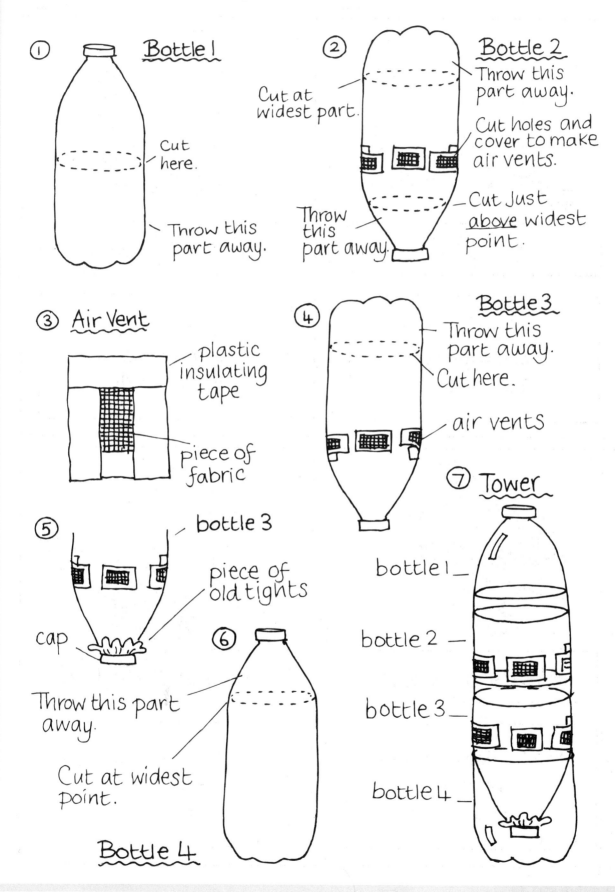

① **Bottle 1**
Cut here.
Throw this part away.

② **Bottle 2**
Cut at widest part.
Throw this part away.
Cut holes and cover to make air vents.
Throw this part away.
Cut just *above* widest point.

③ **Air Vent**
plastic insulating tape
piece of fabric

④ **Bottle 3**
Throw this part away.
Cut here.
air vents

⑤
bottle 3
piece of old tights
cap
Throw this part away.

⑥
Cut at widest point.
Bottle 4

⑦ **Tower**
bottle 1
bottle 2
bottle 3
bottle 4

Name

Date

Brushing your teeth

What I am going to investigate:

How I did my investigation:

How I made it a fair test:

What my tile
looks like:

What happened to the polish on the tile:	What I changed:				

What this test tells me:

Sampling game rules

You have 100 cards, each showing a coloured daisy. Your group needs to find out which colour of daisy is the most common.

1 Sit around a table. Place the cards face down on the table.
2 One at a time, each person picks a card and shows the colour.
3 In the table below, write down the colour. Then the person puts the card back, face down.
4 Now the next person picks a card and shows the colour, and so on.

	What colour was the daisy?
1st go	
2nd go	
3rd go	
4th go	
5th go	
6th go	

5 In your group, try to guess what the most common colour is:

_____

Are you all sure your guess is right?

_____

6 Talk about whether you need to see *all* the cards to find out which is the most common colour. How many would make a good sample? _____

	What colour was the daisy?
7th go	
8th go	
9th go	
10th go	
11th go	
12th go	

7 Before you make a decision about what the most common colour is, sample the cards again. Will this make it easier to decide?

_____

The most common colour is:

_____

Are you all sure your guess is right?

_____

Sampling game cards

Photocopy the sampling cards below to make 100 cards for each group. On each card, colour the middle of the daisy. Within each set of 100 cards, colour 70 blue, 20 red and 10 yellow, for example.

MATERIALS AND THEIR PROPERTIES

It useful to think of 'materials' not always as solids but also as liquids or gases. Simple ingredients found in the kitchen can be used to make interesting materials that children can experience and investigate. These are readily available and are safe for children to use. Investigating familiar materials allows children to discover how important materials are, and how they change, in their everyday lives.

ONE OR TWO SUGARS?

RESOURCES AND CLASSROOM ORGANIZATION

Each group will need:
- various types of sugar e.g. icing sugar, castor sugar, cane sugar, brown sugar, cubed sugar, treacle or syrup, saccharin sweeteners
- containers
- stirrers
- digital weighing scales (in grams)
- water (at room temperature)
- thermometer
- stopwatches/clocks
- 'Investigation planning sheet' – photocopiable page 61
- sticky labels to make badges

INVESTIGATION TYPE:
FAIR TESTING

OBJECTIVES
To develop the following skills:
- turning ideas into a form that can be investigated
- making predictions
- planning a fair test.

VOCABULARY
Dissolving, solution, mixture, stir, soluble, insoluble, sediment.

BACKGROUND KNOWLEDGE

When a substance dissolves, it breaks up into individual particles or molecules. These are spaced throughout the mixture. We call this mixture a solution. When a substance does not dissolve, but mixes into a liquid, it is called a suspension. Emulsion paint and milk are suspensions.

Substances that dissolve in a liquid are described as soluble. Those that do not dissolve are called insoluble.

Substances dissolve more quickly when broken into smaller pieces (larger total surface area), when at a higher temperature and when stirred more frequently.

A soluble substance will continue to dissolve into a liquid until the molecules of the soluble material can no longer find spaces between the molecules of the liquid. At this point, a sediment will remain and the solution is described as saturated.

WHAT TO DO

Brainstorm with the children ideas about sugar and dissolving. Ask them to think about questions that they could investigate, such as those below.
- Do you think different kinds of sugars will all dissolve at the same rate?
- Which sugar will dissolve first?
- Why do you think icing sugar might dissolve first?
- Which sugar will require the smallest number of stirs to dissolve?
- How can we make sure that our test is fair?

Ask each group of children to plan this investigation so that another group can carry it out.

On the 'Investigation planning sheet' (photocopiable page 61), ask the children to identify the variables involved in this investigation. These include volume of water, the rate of stirring, time taken to dissolve, amount of sugar, type of sugar, shape of the container, temperature.

Explain that they are going to measure how long it takes each type of sugar to dissolve completely. Therefore, they should only change the type of sugar, and all the other variables should be kept the same. It can be difficult to keep the rate of stirring the same, but if the children try to give one complete stir each second this should

give a fairly constant rate. To keep the temperature constant, use lukewarm water at room temperature, rather than cold water fresh from the tap or heated water that will rapidly cool. The children might want to check the temperature so a thermometer should be made available.

When the groups have completed their planning, ask them to swap their planning sheets with another group. Each group should then make predictions about what they think is going to happen, based on the questions from the initial brainstorm.

Ask the children to carry out the investigation based on the planning sheet they have been given. They can make adjustments to the investigation, but these must be reported back to the original group at the end of the activity.

A large amount of sugar will take ages to dissolve so encourage the children to use small amounts. They can accurately weigh a few grams of sugar using digital scales. If these are not available, use half a teaspoon.

As the children carry out the investigation they should record their results and once they have finished they should present their results as a bar graph.

In their conclusions, the children should:
■ make positive and constructive comments about the planning they have used
■ relate their results to their predictions; how are the results similar or different?
■ give possible explanations for the results
■ explain how they have answered the questions from the brainstorm.

SAFETY

If the children want to go on to investigate the effects of temperature on dissolving rate, water from a hot tap should be sufficiently warm. Never use boiling water.

DIFFERENTIATION

More able children could plan and carry out an investigation to find out how changing other variables affects the rate at which sugar dissolves.

Children who are not able to deal with thinking about lots of variables could investigate how much sugar will dissolve in a fixed amount of water.

NOW OR LATER

■ Children could test various materials to see if they are soluble or insoluble.
Children could collect various cooking ingredients and sort them into groups based on their solubilities.
■ Children could investigate whether the shape or size of a tea bag really makes a difference to the rate at which the tea dissolves.

PHLUBBER!!

RESOURCES AND CLASSROOM ORGANIZATION

Each group will need:
- ingredients to make 'phlubber': talcum powder (e.g. baby powder), oil-free moisturizer (e.g. baby lotion), PVA glue, 5% borax solution, water
- paper cup
- stirrer
- teaspoon (5ml measure)
- goggles.

BACKGROUND KNOWLEDGE

'Phlubber' is a material that can be described as a fluid, as it will flow and will eventually take the shape of its container. The word 'fluid' is used to describe not just liquids but also gases and some apparently solid materials like hair gel, toothpaste and tomato ketchup.

We can imagine materials like this to be made of long particles, which are linked firmly together. A material like 'phlubber' will behave in different ways depending on the force applied to it. When a sudden force is applied – when it is dropped on the floor or hit, for example – then the particles bend and act like springs, so the 'phlubber' will bounce. If a strong force is applied, as when the 'phlubber' is pulled suddenly, the links between the particles snap and the 'phlubber' breaks. When the force is applied slowly, the particles separate and form new links so the 'phlubber' stretches and flows.

WHAT TO DO

Divide the class into small groups. Each child can make some 'phlubber', as described below. Show the ingredients to the children, and describe them and what they are used for. Ask the children what they think would happen if they mixed these ingredients together? What would the new substance look like? Would it be soft, sticky, runny? Ask them to record their ideas.

To make 'phlubber', measure out one level teaspoon of talcum powder and place it in the paper cup. Add 10cm³ of moisturizer, 10cm³ of PVA glue and 10cm³ of water. Stir well to mix the ingredients.

Add 5cm³ of borax solution and stir. (Borax can be obtained from most pharmacies. To make a 5% solution, mix 5ml of borax into 100ml of water. You may need to vary the concentration to obtain the best results.)

Remove the 'phlubber' from the cup. Are the children surprised at the 'new' material they have made? How is it different from their expectations?

Children could investigate the following questions and record their observations.
- Is there a difference between pulling hard on the 'phlubber', and stretching it slowly?
- How does the shape of the 'phlubber' affect the way it bounces? (You could try bouncing ball shapes, sausage shapes, or flattened pieces of 'phlubber'.)
- What happens when you leave a ball of 'phlubber' on a surface?
- What happens when you leave a ball of 'phlubber' in a container?
- Compare 'phlubber' to other similar substances, such as Blu-Tack and Plasticine.

SAFETY

Goggles are recommended, but otherwise there are no safety hazards in using these materials.

OBJECTIVES

To develop the following skills:
- observation skills
- developing ideas and questions
- following instructions
- using knowledge and understanding to develop ideas about a 'new' material.

VOCABULARY

Stretching, material, properties, bounce, fluid, flow.

37

DIFFERENTIATION

This activity can be extended by asking the children to investigate the effect of changing the concentration of borax on the rate at which 'phlubber' flows. To measure the flow rate, a ball of 'phlubber' is placed on a surface marked with concentric circles spaced at centimetre intervals. The time it takes to spread from one circle to the next is measured and recorded.

NOW OR LATER

Children can investigate other materials, such as cornflour or silly putty, which stiffen when stirred. They could also look at materials such as toothpaste and tomato ketchup, which flow more quickly when a force is applied.

To investigate cornflour, add the water to the cornflour powder (never the other way around) in a container, and stir. Produce a mixture with a runny consistency.

Try investigating what happens when you stir quickly then slowly. Hit the mixture with your fingers. How does this feel? Now push your fingers slowly into the mixture. Do you notice any difference?

To investigate silly putty, mix $20cm^3$ of PVA glue with $20cm^3$ of water in a paper cup. Add $5cm^3$ of borax solution. Stir the mixture, then remove it from the cup and knead it with your fingers. Great fun.

Children can compare the behaviour of this material to that of 'phlubber'.

AMAZING RAISINS

OBJECTIVES

To develop the following skills:
■ relating observations to scientific knowledge and understanding to explain a range of everyday changes
■ using observations to describe changes
■ identifying new materials based on evidence.

VOCABULARY

Reversible, irreversible, dissolve, carbon dioxide.

RESOURCES AND CLASSROOM ORGANIZATION

Each group will need:
■ water
■ vinegar
■ bicarbonate of soda (baking powder)
■ raisins
■ clear plastic or glass jar with a lid
■ teaspoon (5ml measure)
■ goggles.

BACKGROUND KNOWLEDGE

A chemical reaction takes place between vinegar and bicarbonate of soda. One of the products of that reaction is the gas carbon dioxide (CO_2). This is insoluble in water, so it forms bubbles. If there are raisins in the reaction mixture, some of the bubbles attach themselves to the rough surface of the raisins, making them buoyant. This makes them rise to the surface. Here the bubbles of carbon dioxide burst and escape into the air. This decreases the buoyancy of the raisins, so they sink. This process will continue until all the bicarbonate of soda has reacted with the vinegar.

Children need to understand that this is an example of an irreversible reaction and that the bicarbonate of soda has changed into a new substance – in this case a kind of salt – because it has lost carbon dioxide.

WHAT TO DO

Fill the jar two thirds full of water. Ask the children to predict what will happen when vinegar and bicarbonate of soda are added. Add a little vinegar (60ml) and two teaspoons (10ml) of bicarbonate of soda. Stir gently. The children should record what they observe – they should notice that bubbles are produced.

Ask the children what will happen when a few raisins are added. Then add the raisins. As long as their surfaces stay fairly rough, they should begin to bounce up and down. Put the lid on the jar to make the effect last longer. The children should record their observations.

Ask the children to think about these questions. Record their ideas as they answer.
- What are the bubbles?
- Where have they come from?
- What effect do they have on the raisins?
- How can we find out what is making them?

SAFETY

Children should learn to handle all substances carefully. They should wash their hands to avoid any of these substances coming in contact with their eyes. Goggles are recommended for these investigations.

NOW OR LATER

- Children could find out what other substances will react with bicarbonate of soda to produce carbon dioxide; for example, lemon and orange juice, cold tea. These substances are called acids.
- Children could devise an investigation to find out for how long a teaspoon of bicarbonate of soda will produce bubbles in a fixed amount of vinegar solution. Will two teaspoons last twice as long? Is there a pattern, so that we could predict how long ten teaspoons would produce bubbles for?
- Bubble power: *do this teacher-only demonstration outside and wear safety goggles.* Place a small amount of vinegar in a film canister, and put in one Alka-Seltzer tablet, quickly and firmly replacing the lid. Stand back. After a few moments the lid should fly off with a loud 'pop' and foam should bubble out of the canister.

DRYING THE WASHING

RESOURCES AND CLASSROOM ORGANIZATION

Each group will need:
- paper towels
- water
- large flat tray
- measuring beakers or measuring cylinders
- pegs
- string for a washing line
- stopwatches/clocks.

It is advisable to plan ahead and to find out approximately how long the paper towels you will be using take to dry.

BACKGROUND KNOWLEDGE

Evaporation is the term given to the process by which a liquid changes into a gas at a temperature below the liquid's boiling point. Evaporation takes place at the surface of the liquid. So the larger the surface area, the greater the chance of evaporation taking place. Moving molecules at the surface of the liquid escape into the air, and any activity that increases this movement, such as an increase in the surrounding temperature or air movements across the surface of the liquid, will increase the rate at which the liquid evaporates.

INVESTIGATION TYPE:
FAIR TESTING

OBJECTIVES

To develop the following skills:
- planning a fair test
- making repeated measurements
- making predictions
- assessing how well the evidence supports the prediction.

VOCABULARY

Evaporation, rate of evaporation, surface area, liquid, gas, process, saturated, water vapour.

Evaporation is a physical change and is reversible. The reverse process is called condensation. Both play an important role in the water cycle.

WHAT TO DO

Ask the children what they think happens to the water in puddles after it rains. Ask them to think about why washing dries – where does the water go? What happens to it? Ask the children to record their ideas in picture form.

Ask the children what they think will make washing dry faster or slower. They should identify variables such as how wet the washing is (the volume of water that has to evaporate), the temperature, how windy it is and the size and shape of the item of washing (its surface area). Explain to the children that they are going to investigate the question 'Do large things dry more quickly or more slowly than small things?' So they will be varying the size, or surface area, of the 'washing', but they need to keep the other variables the same in order to make it a fair test.

They should use the same amount of water each time; for example, 25ml.

Setting up the investigation in the classroom or practical area should ensure that the temperature and wind speed are controlled.

Ask the children to make 'clothes' out of paper towels. They need to make items with certain values of surface area; for example, $100cm^2$, $150cm^2$, $200cm^2$, $250cm^2$, $300cm^2$. To do this, ask the children to draw their 'clothes' shapes on centimetre-squared paper so that they cover the right number of squares. They can then cut these out and use them as templates to draw around on the paper towels, cutting the final 'clothes' items out of the paper towels. Organize the class into groups so that each group has three examples of each surface area value. The children then soak each sample in a tray containing a measured volume of water, and hang it on a washing line.

The children then time how long it takes for the samples to dry. They can get an indication of when a sample is dry by comparing the colour with that of a dry paper towel. Each group records their three repeated readings and calculates the average drying time for each surface area. Data is collected from each group to produce a table that shows all the class results. This can be used to plot graphs either as a class or individually.

If a line graph is constructed, with time plotted against surface area, the children should be able to observe a pattern that enables them to make statements in their conclusions such as 'The bigger the surface area the faster the water evaporates.'

They may be able to extend the line and infer how quickly the same volume of water might evaporate from other larger or smaller samples. They should also be able to work out how quickly samples with surface areas between the values used would dry.

If a bar graph is produced, the children will be able to make comparisons between samples and can make statements such as 'The biggest surface area dries the quickest'.

DIFFERENTIATION

Less able children may find it easier to work with just three samples, each of a different size, soaking them all with the same amount of water. They can then compare the samples as they dry.

More able children could be asked to investigate other factors that might affect the rate of evaporation, such as temperature, wind speed (could be varied using a fan) or type of material.

NOW OR LATER

■ After it has rained, children could draw with chalk around puddles, and repeat this process at regular intervals until the puddle has completely evaporated. They will be able to observe how the size of the puddle has reduced. By pouring water back into the puddle and measuring how much it takes to reach each interval mark, the children will be able to work out how much water has evaporated during each time interval, and thereby calculate the rate of evaporation.

■ Children could look at how the process of evaporation can be used to reclaim a dissolved substance such as salt. They could use this phenomenon to explain why rain is not salty.

SILLY MIXTURE

INVESTIGATION TYPE:
EXPLORING

RESOURCES AND CLASSROOM ORGANIZATION

Each group will need:
■ a mixture of salt, water, sand, iron filings, marbles and sawdust or wood shavings
■ a plastic container
■ a spoon
■ plastic saucers, to allow substances to dry or evaporate
■ a magnet
■ sieves
■ goggles.

OBJECTIVES

To develop the following skills:
■ using knowledge and understanding of separation techniques
■ exploring how the properties of materials determine how they can be separated
■ planning, recording and making decisions.

VOCABULARY

Separation, evaporation, sieving, sedimentation, magnetic, condensation, filtration.

BACKGROUND KNOWLEDGE

In this activity, all of the substances listed above are mixed together, and the children are asked to work out how to separate them. One way of doing this is by following the sequence below.

1 Sieve the mixture using a fine sieve to remove solid materials, and allow them to dry naturally.

2 A clear salt solution remains after sieving; allow the water to evaporate, leaving solid salt. (Explain to the children that the water could be recovered too, by boiling the solution and then condensing the water vapour produced, but that this would be very difficult and dangerous to do in class. However, the water that has evaporated will return next time it rains!)

3 Use a large sieve to remove the marbles from the mixture of dry solid materials (or you could simply pick them out by hand).

MARINO INSTITUTE OF EDUCATION

4 Use a magnet to remove the iron filings from the mixture. (If you cover the magnet in paper or clingfilm first, it makes the iron filings easier to get off afterwards!)
5 Only the sand and sawdust or wood shavings now remain; mix them in water and allow them to settle (this is sedimentation). The wood should float and can be scooped out with a spoon. Carefully pour the water away (or sieve the mixture again), and let the sand dry.

WHAT TO DO

Prepare the mixture; dissolve a quantity of the salt into the water and then add all the other materials. Use small plastic containers (500ml) to distribute a sample of the mixture to each group.

Explain to the children that you have a problem: all these materials have fallen into a container of water and you need to get them all back. Ask them to suggest ways in which they could separate all the materials in the mixture. They need to think about the different properties of the materials, and the order in which to use the various separation techniques.

Ask the children to record their ideas using notes. They should use their notes to try to actually solve the problem. During the investigation, they should also make notes of any changes that they have made to their ideas or problems they have encountered.

Once they have solved the problem, the children can record their solution using pictures and notes, describing what they did and what equipment and techniques they used. These records could be made into a book.

SAFETY

Iron filings and sawdust can pose a risk to eyes. It encourages good practice for children to wear goggles when working with any such material in science.

In the primary classroom, it is highly inadvisable to attempt to separate the water from the filtered salt solution by boiling it and condensing the water vapour produced back into water.

DIFFERENTIATION

More able children might find it more of a challenge if they are not told that there is salt dissolved in the mixture, but instead are encouraged to think about the fact that a clear liquid might still be a mixture in itself. Cooking oil or gravel could also be added to the mixture to provide an extra challenge.

NOW OR LATER

■ A description of this challenge could be incorporated into a creative writing story, in which children have to solve the problem in the style of an 'Indiana Jones' action adventure.
■ Children could use reference materials to find out how various separation processes are used in everyday life.
■ Arrange a visit to a local sewage plant or industrial plant to see how they use separation processes.

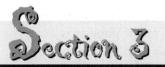

PHYSICAL PROCESSES

The physical world provides ideal opportunities for investigations and with the use of simple measuring equipment children are able to collect numerical data. This can be turned into graphs, analysed and possible trends and patterns identified.

PUSH-PULL-O-METER

INVESTIGATION TYPE:
MAKING THINGS

RESOURCES AND CLASSROOM ORGANIZATION
Each group (or each child, if resources allow) will need:
- a cotton reel
- 15–20cm length of dowel (0.5cm in diameter, to fit through a cotton reel)
- insulating tape
- paper clips
- rubber bands
- 100g weights (masses)
- margarine tub, or similar container
- collection of objects for testing (of various weights, but small enough to fit in the container)
- string.

BACKGROUND KNOWLEDGE
Children need to know that 100g exerts a force of 1 newton (N); it has a weight of 1N. So it requires a force of 1N to lift it. The weight of an object is a force, and is dependent on the mass of the object and the gravitational force acting upon it.

The newton is the standard (SI) unit for force, named after the famous scientist Sir Isaac Newton.

Friction is the scientific name given to the force that resists the movement of one surface against another. It is caused by surfaces being covered with microscopic bumps, however smooth they feel or look. These bumps interact with one another, locking together. The more of these connections that have to be broken in order for the surfaces to move, the more energy, and so the greater the force is required. Lubricants help to prevent this locking together, so allowing the surfaces to move more freely. Friction also occurs when objects travel through air or water.

WHAT TO DO
Tell the children that they are going to make their own measuring device to measure pushes and pulls. Use the step-by-step instructions given below.
1 Cut the elastic band, and tape it to the cotton reel.
2 Push through the dowel rod and tape it to the elastic band.
3 Tape a paper clip to the end of the dowel to make a hook.
4 To calibrate the push-pull-o-meter, hold the cotton reel upright as shown overleaf, and

OBJECTIVES
To develop the following skills:
- making measurements using a force meter
- recognizing that a push and a pull are opposing forces
- measuring forces using standard units
- using scientific knowledge to make a measuring device
- developing the concept that friction is a force that opposes the movement of objects.

VOCABULARY
Force, measure, calibrate, newtons.

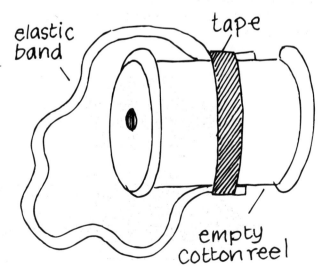

elastic band

tape

empty cotton reel

hang a 100g mass on the hook. Mark the dowel level with the top of the cotton reel, and label the mark 'IN'. Repeat this using increasing masses, up to about 500g (5N).

5 Use the end with the paper clip to measure pulls; the other end of the dowel can be used to measure pushes.

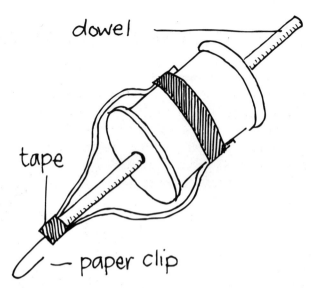

Ask the children to make a collection of objects. One at time, they should place each object in a margarine tub, or similar container, on the surface of a table. Ask the children to estimate how many Newtons it will take to push or pull the object along the surface of the table, in the container. Will the size of the force required to push it be the same as the force needed to pull it? What reasons do they give?

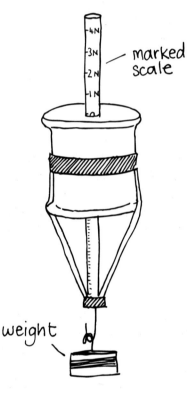

Now ask the children to use their push-pull-o-meter to find the force needed to pull or push each object. Were their predictions correct?

Ask the children to weigh each object, to see if there is a relationship between the weight and the force required to move the object.

Using string, suspend the container so that it no longer rests on the table surface. Ask the children to test the objects again – is there a difference in the amount of force needed to move each of them? Ask the children to offer a possible explanation for this. This will help to start the children thinking about friction as a force between two surfaces, which acts in opposition to a push or pull in a given direction.

SAFETY
Children need to take care if they are to cut the dowel to size. Some tape around the end of the paper clip will prevent the risk of injury.

NOW OR LATER
■ Children could design a fair test to investigate the effects of moving an object over different surfaces. They could use their own push-pull-o-meter to take measurements, or use a real force meter. Force meters are available with different sized springs in them so that they can be used to measure the force required to move heavier objects.
■ Children could use reference materials to find out how friction is important to us; how it is used to advantage (in the brakes on a bike, for example) and how we reduce it when it is an inconvenience (using oil on the chain of a bike, for example).
■ Children could write a poem about friction. If friction were a person, what would he or she be like? How would the person behave? What would his or her character be like?

HOW OLD WOULD I BE ON VENUS?

RESOURCES AND CLASSROOM ORGANIZATION

This investigation can be divided into activities, which can be completed separately or together. One activity involves investigating data using ICT, and the other is a practical activity. In both parts, the children construct models of the Solar System.
Each group will need:
■ string
■ stopwatch/clock
■ metre ruler
■ a ball or sphere to attach to string
■ access to a computer, with a spreadsheet program
■ 'Planet information' sheet – photocopiable page 58
■ 'Investigation planning sheet' – photocopiable page 61
■ 'Data recording sheet' – photocopiable page 62
■ 'Keeping it safe!' sheet – photocopiable page 63

BACKGROUND KNOWLEDGE

Children will need to have some understanding of the force of gravity and that the gravitational pull of the Sun is holding all the planets of our Solar System in orbit around it. If the Sun stopped exerting a gravitational pull, each planet would move away in a straight line. This can be easily illustrated by swinging a ball attached to string round in a circle, and watching what happens when you let go of the string. Most planetary orbits, however, are not circular, like the orbit of the ball on the string, but elliptical.

WHAT TO DO

Begin with a class discussion about birthdays and age, and lead into how we measure a year on the planet Earth. (Further discussion may be needed about orbits and the planet's position in the Solar System.) Ask the children to research the question 'Do all the planets take the same time to orbit the Sun?'

The class can then use various research materials – such as books, videos, CD-ROMs and the Internet – to find the information required. They can construct a table of data. If research materials are unavailable, use the 'Planet information' sheet on photocopiable page 58.

From this data conclusions can be drawn and the following statement constructed: 'The further away a planet is from the Sun, the longer it takes to orbit the Sun'.

Here the investigation can be divided into two activities – one ICT-based, and the other a practical investigation.

ICT INVESTIGATION

Set up a simple model in a spreadsheet model, as described below:
1 In your spreadsheet, copy row 1 as shown overleaf.
2 Copy the data into columns A and B as shown overleaf.
3 Move to cell C2 and enter your age.
4 Move to cell C3 and enter the following formula: =ROUND(C2/B3,2)
This works out your age on Mercury, in 'Mercury years'.
5 Copy cell C3.
6 Paste it into cells C4 to C11. This calculates your age on all planets, in 'planet years'.

OBJECTIVES
To develop the following skills:
■ using and refining concepts about orbits, gravity, time scales and the Solar System through models
■ constructing a table of data
■ using reference material and secondary sources
■ using ICT
■ using simple equipment
■ making careful and repeated observations and measurements.

VOCABULARY
Orbits, planets, spreadsheet, model, gravity, Solar System.

The results will provide many opportunities to discuss data. For example, what does '17.74 years' mean? To convert to years and months, first take off the whole number (17 in this case) – this is the number of years. Then take the decimal part (0.74) and multiply it by 12. So 17.74 years becomes 17 years and 8 months.

	A	B	C
1	PLANET	PLANET ORBIT TIME (in Earth years)	Age (in planet years)
2	EARTH	1	11
3	MERCURY	0.24	45.83
4	VENUS	0.62	17.74
5	MARS	1.88	5.85
6	JUPITER	11.86	0.93
7	SATURN	29.46	0.37
8	URANUS	84.01	0.13
9	NEPTUNE	184.79	0.07
10	PLUTO	247.70	0.04

From the spreadsheet, the children can produce a bar graph. They could write a series of questions to answer using the graph, which could be displayed and used by the whole class; for example, 'How old would you be on Venus?'

Notice that the orbit times given for each planet are measured in Earth years – if they were measured in each planet's definition of a year, all the orbit times would of course be '1'. By the same token, the ages on each planet are calculated by the spreadsheet model in terms of each planet's definition of a year – if they were given in Earth years, they would all be the same as the age on Earth.

PRACTICAL INVESTIGATION

In this activity, the children investigate the question 'Do planets that are further from the Sun take longer to orbit?'

Attach a ball or small mass to the end of a piece of string. The ball represents a planet; the string represents the gravitational pull of the Sun. Ask the children to swing the ball around their heads to represent an orbit. What do they notice as they lengthen the string?

Discuss with the children that they are going to change the length of the string and measure how long it takes for the ball to cover ten revolutions past a fixed point. Decisions need to be made about the range of string lengths to be used; 25–150cm will be adequate. Copies of the 'Investigation planning sheet' (photocopiable page 61) can be used.

The children should record the lengths of string used and the time taken for each set of ten revolutions. Encourage the children to take repeated readings and to use averages. They can record this on the 'Data recording sheet' (photocopiable page 62). From their data, they can produce a line graph, plotting the average time for ten revolutions (or for a single orbit, if they divide by ten) on the (vertical) y-axis, against the length of the string on the (horizontal) x-axis. The conclusions children draw from the data should support their previous research, and confirm that 'The further away a planet is from the Sun, the longer it takes to orbit the Sun'.

SAFETY

The practical activity must take place outside, and the children should be aware of the safety issue raised by swinging an object when other people are around. Ask the children to use the 'Keeping it safe!' sheet (photocopiable page 63) to assess the risks involved and to decide what actions to take.

NOW OR LATER

■ The idea of time and space is a complex one, but it can be an excellent stimulus for creative writing and poetry.
■ Use a spreadsheet program to create other models of the Solar System; for example, look at how the size of a planet is related to its distance from the Sun.
■ Try to construct a scale model of the planets and their distances from the Sun, which will help to give the children some idea of the immense scale of the Solar System. Use the data and suggestions on the 'Planet information' sheet (photocopiable sheet 58) – note that you will need a huge space, such as the school field, if you wish to represent accurately the distances between the planets.
■ Some CD-ROM encyclopaedias have activities with which the children can interact to find out more about how the Solar System works; for example, Microsoft Encarta has an excellent simulation about orbits.

HELICOPTERS

RESOURCES AND CLASSROOM ORGANIZATION

Each group (or each child, if resources allow) will need:
■ 'Make a helicopter' sheet – photocopiable page 59
■ paper clips
■ scissors
■ stopwatches/clocks
■ different types of paper e.g. tissue, drawing, activity, card, paper towel
■ 'Investigation planning sheet' – photocopiable page 61
■ 'Data recording sheet' – photocopiable page 62.

BACKGROUND KNOWLEDGE

Objects fall because they are being pulled towards the centre of the Earth by a force called gravity. The rate at which an object falls depends upon its shape, which affects the air resistance as it falls. It does *not* depend upon the mass of the object; heavy and light objects would fall at the same rate if there were no air resistance.

The wings of the paper helicopter (see photocopiable page 59) offer resistance to the air. This provides an opposing force to gravity, so slowing the rate at which the helicopter falls. It is impossible to increase the air resistance sufficiently to stop the object falling at all by increasing the size of the wings, as this also increases the mass of the object. This means it requires an even greater force to keep it from falling. In order for an object to remain suspended in the air, additional forces are required. In aeroplanes and helicopters, lift produced as the wings or rotor blades move through the air provides this force, while gliders use the force from rising air currents.

WHAT TO DO

This activity provides an ideal opportunity for children to make many decisions about what to investigate and the type of investigation they want to carry out. The children should be encouraged to use the findings from their initial investigations to produce questions to prompt further investigations. From this activity, it should be expected that the children will perhaps undertake at least two investigations, the first prompting the second.

INVESTIGATION TYPE:
THE CHILDREN DECIDE:
EXPLORING, MAKING THINGS,
FAIR TESTING OR PATTERN
SEEKING

OBJECTIVES

To develop the following skills:
■ using focused exploration and investigation to acquire scientific knowledge and skills
■ turning ideas into a form that can be investigated
■ deciding upon a suitable method of investigation.

VOCABULARY

Air resistance, gravity, force, clockwise, anti-clockwise.

EXPLORING

Ask the children to make helicopters as shown on photocopiable page 59. Once they have made them, they can suggest what might happen when they drop the helicopters. Will they float or spin? Which way will they spin? The children should then drop the helicopters and record their observations.

The children can then make changes to the helicopters, and see how their flight is affected. What happens when they add more paper clips, or fold the wings the other way, or drop them from a different height?

The children can record their ideas pictorially and make detailed notes. From these, they can devise further questions that could be investigated.

MAKING THINGS

Children could investigate the ways in which 'flying' devices are made. They could modify the design of the helicopter, perhaps using different materials such as tissue paper, card or corrugated plastic. Through research, children could look at other designs for 'flying' devices, such as frisbees, paper planes and parachutes. The children should record and present their designs with detailed notes explaining their modifications.

This activity could lead to the children designing a fair test investigation to identify the most effective design.

FAIR TESTING

Children could use the 'Investigation planning sheet' (photocopiable page 61) to brainstorm the variables they could change in order to investigate the factors affecting the way the paper helicopter flies. These could include the number of paper clips, the height of drop, the length of the wings and the width of the wings. Children could measure the effects of changing these variables on the number of spins or the time the helicopter takes to drop.

Once the children have identified the variables they are going to change, and what they are going to measure, they need to keep all the other variables the same in order to make it a fair test. Before the children carry out the investigation, ask them to make predictions about what might happen. During the investigation, the children should make repeated measurements and calculate averages, which can be recorded on the 'Data recording sheet' (photocopiable page 62). The results can be plotted on a graph.

Children need opportunities to discuss their results. What does the evidence tell them? How does it relate to their predictions? Ask them to make a statement about their investigation; for example, 'My evidence shows that when I increase the number of paper clips on my helicopter it falls more quickly – the heavier the helicopter, the faster it starts to fall'. The children should try to offer explanations for this finding based on their scientific knowledge and understanding.

This investigation leads very nicely into investigating patterns in data.

PATTERN SEEKING

To undertake this investigation, the children must either already have carried out a fair test, or use data from another group who have carried out a fair test investigation. The children should look at the data, and plot a graph. They should look to see if there is any pattern in the data. Can they predict from the data what will happen next by extending the graph? For example, can they predict how quickly the helicopter will start to fall if it has six or seven paper clips attached? What if it has three and a half paper clips? The children should record their ideas along with their evidence. They can produce a report that offers possible explanations for the patterns and suggests what further investigations they could undertake.

SAFETY

Children should be aware of the risk involved if they are standing on a chair or other platform to drop their helicopters.

DIFFERENTIATION

More able children could undertake a project to investigate the helicopter using all four methods. They could decide which approach to start with and from the conclusions decide what to investigate next.

Less able children will need to have an approach suggested to them, selected by the teacher according to ability.

NOW OR LATER

This activity can be broken down into modules, during each of which the class investigate using a different approach. It could take place over a whole year, and when it is finished the class could put on a display and demonstration of their work for other children and parents.

ME AND MY SHADOW

INVESTIGATION TYPES:
FAIR TESTING AND PATTERN SEEKING

RESOURCES AND CLASSROOM ORGANIZATION

This activity must take place in a darkened room to obtain the best results. Tape a large sheet of paper to a wall as a screen, and place the light source about 1m away. Use an opaque object to cast a shadow. To help measure the distance between the light source and the wall, use masking tape on a table; marking at 10cm intervals.

Each group will need:
- 'Investigation planning sheet' – photocopiable page 61
- 'Data recording sheet' – photocopiable page 62
- a regularly shaped opaque object
- a light source e.g. torch or projector
- a large sheet of paper
- masking tape
- rulers
- a metre stick.

OBJECTIVES

To develop the following skills:
- planning and carrying out a fair test
- making a prediction and comparing it to the findings
- making observations and taking measurements
- presenting results as a line graph
- identifying patterns in data.

VOCABULARY

Light, beam, shadow, length, opaque, distance, prediction.

BACKGROUND KNOWLEDGE

Light travels in straight lines at a speed of 299,792,458 m/s. It spreads out from a source, so the position and size of a shadow can be predicted. The shadow gets larger as the distance between the object and the screen increases (or when the distance between the object and the light source decreases).

WHAT TO DO

Ask the children how they think shadows are formed. What is involved? Do shadows change size? Why do they think this happens?

Set up the apparatus as described above, with the light source about 1m from a screen on the wall. Explain to the children that they are going change the distance between an object and the screen, and that they are going to measure the height of the shadow each time they do so. Ask them to record their predictions about how the shadow might change. This can be done in a number of ways. The children could just make a statement such as 'The further the object is from the screen the bigger the shadow is'. Or they could try to quantify their statement by saying something like 'When it is half way it will be twice the size'. The children could quantify their predictions further by estimating what size the shadow will be when the object is at each 10cm mark. They could record these predictions in a table, and produce a line graph to be compared later with the final results. Which way do they predict the graph will slope? Will it be a straight line, curvy line or wobbly line?

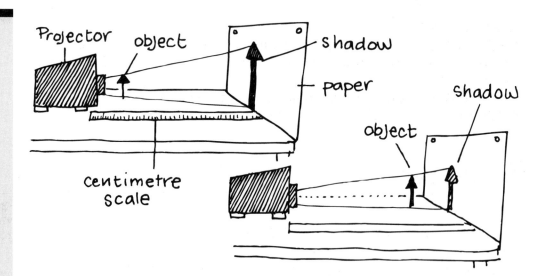

The children should then carry out the investigation, recording their results. They will find it easier to measure the height of the shadow by marking the top on the paper on the wall and measuring that distance once the object is removed. This is easier than trying to hold the object still while the shadow itself is measured.

Once the children have collected their evidence, they can compare the results to their predictions, and record any differences. How has this investigation changed their thinking? This is an ideal opportunity to discuss with the children the concept of making a prediction. Many children are desperate to find the 'correct' answer. This often limits their thinking. Make the children aware that a prediction is about thinking what might happen and as good scientists they need to think of as many possible outcomes as they can.

The children should produce a line graph from their results, showing the height of the shadow on the (vertical) y-axis plotted against the distance from the wall on the (horizontal) x-axis. What do they notice about the graph? What is its shape? What does this say about light and shadows? Ask them to record and present their ideas.

The children should notice from their results and observations that the size of the shadow changes slowly as you bring the object away from the wall, but then starts to increase more quickly for each 10cm increase in distance from the screen. The line will therefore start to rise quite gently, but then become steeper (see below).

SAFETY

Projectors present some risks, as they are mains operated, and contain glass and hot, bright bulbs. Highlight the possible risks and warn the children not to look directly at the bright light. Remind them that they must take responsibility for their own safety and that of others when using this equipment.

DIFFERENTIATION

More able children could devise their own fair test investigation by identifying and changing another variable and observing the effect this has on the shadow. They could, for example, change the angle of the light source, the transparency, width or height of the object, or the brightness of the surrounding light.

Less able children could record the height of the shadow using strips of paper cut to size. They could then stick these at 10cm intervals along a metre line drawn on a large sheet of paper. This would give a visual representation of their results.

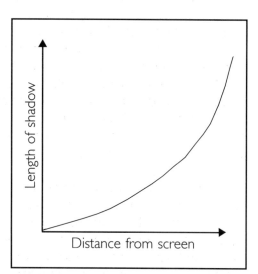

NOW OR LATER

1 Make sundials and calibrate them so that they can be used to tell the time.
2 Record how shadows change due to the apparent movement of the Sun across the sky.
3 Make shadow puppets and produce a small play to perform.
4 Make silhouettes of the children's profiles.

STRETCHING

RESOURCES AND CLASSROOM ORGANIZATION

Each group will need:
■ elastic band (use the same length and thickness for the whole class)
■ weights or masses
■ paper clip
■ string
■ light container such as yoghurt pot
■ goggles
■ 'Data recording sheet' – photocopiable page 62.

BACKGROUND KNOWLEDGE

In the apparatus shown, gravity pulls the weight down. As it does this, it applies a force to the elastic band. The rubber material from which this is made stretches, and applies an opposing force stopping the weight from falling. Once the weight is removed the material returns to its normal size. As larger weights are added, the elastic band stretches more, until enough weight is added to stretch the material to its maximum. Beyond this point the material will break.

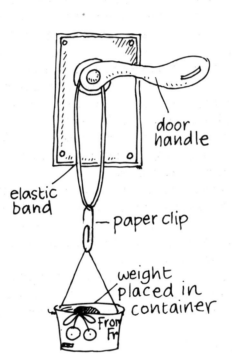

In many cases, the stretch of a material is proportional to the force pulling it. This was discovered by a scientist called Robert Hooke and is called 'Hooke's Law'.

WHAT TO DO

Discuss with the children the properties of elastic bands – how they stretch and then spring back to their original shape.

Measure the length of the elastic band. Hang it from a secure fixture such as a door handle, with a light container attached, as shown in the diagram above. Mark where the lower end of the band reaches, using chalk. Gently add a fixed weight such as 100g (1N). (This weight should be decided by the teacher beforehand, taking into account the properties of the elastic bands used.) The elastic band will stretch. The children can then measure the new length of the band. Another elastic band is added on to the secure fixture and the weight attached to both elastic bands. Can the children predict what will happen? The process is repeated until the bands no longer stretch.

The children can record their results on the 'Data recording sheet' (photocopiable page 62) and from these results produce a bar graph. They should look to see if there is a pattern between the number of bands and the distance they stretch, and construct a statement about their findings. They also might like to think about how elastic bands and other materials are woven together to give extra strength; for example, in ropes and string, steel cable and bungee ropes.

INVESTIGATION TYPE:
PATTERN SEEKING

OBJECTIVES

To develop the following skills:
■ carrying out a fair test
■ making predictions
■ making observations and taking measurements
■ presenting results as a graph
■ identifying patterns in data
■ using knowledge and understanding to explain findings.

VOCABULARY

Stretch, weight, pull, measure, force, limit, longer, newton, elastic.

Ready to go! IDEAS FOR SCIENCE INVESTIGATIONS

SAFETY

There is a risk that the elastic bands might snap so it is important that the children wear goggles during this activity. The children also need to take care that the weights do not fall onto their toes. A box placed under the apparatus will keep feet out of danger, and prevent damage to the floor.

DIFFERENTIATION

More able children could try to devise their own questions about the stretching behaviour of elastic bands, and to identify what variables they need to change in order to investigate their questions in a fair test.

Less able children could collect a variety of materials and explore how far they stretch. They could order or group the materials according to their 'stretchiness'.

NOW OR LATER

■ Children could investigate Hooke's Law by repeating the investigation. This time, instead of changing the number of bands, they could change the weight or mass attached to a band and measure the distance it stretches. Children need to take care with this activity, as the bands will eventually break.

■ Children could make stretchy dough. What effect does changing the amounts of water and flour have on the dough's stretchiness?

BALLS AND BOUNCING

INVESTIGATION TYPE:
FAIR TESTING

OBJECTIVES

To develop the following skills:
■ making predictions
■ developing ideas about fair testing
■ producing a table and graph of results
■ making comparisons
■ identifying patterns in data
■ reviewing predictions and ideas based on evidence.

VOCABULARY

Height, bounce, plastic, sponge, squashy, hard, material.

RESOURCES AND CLASSROOM ORGANIZATION

This investigation describes in detail how to carry out a fair test. Teachers can use it as an example of the process of fair testing, so the elements can be applied to any other investigations.

The activity can be organized in a variety of ways. It can be carried out in small groups or individually. Or a combination of various methods can be used. So, for example, the children may plan as individuals, identifying variables and making predictions; then work in small groups to carry out the investigation, collecting and recording data. Then results could be discussed and reviewed as a class, finally returning to an individual activity to describe children's conclusions and findings. By using a combination of classroom organization techniques, difficulties posed by lack of resources and by the need to identify children's individual achievements can be addressed.

Each group (or each child, if resources allow) will need:
■ various types of ball, made from different materials and ranging from hard to soft e.g. golf ball, tennis ball, ping-pong ball, sponge ball, bouncy ball, cricket ball
■ a metre ruler or measuring tape
■ access to a variety of floor coverings e.g. hard floor tile, cork tile, carpet, grass, concrete, tarmac
■ 'Investigation planning sheet' – photocopiable page 61
■ 'Data recording sheet' – photocopiable page 62

BACKGROUND KNOWLEDGE

Balls bounce due to their elasticity. When a ball is held up in the air it has stored or potential energy. When you let go and drop it, this stored energy is changed into movement or kinetic energy. The force of hitting the floor changes the shape of the ball. The

elasticity of the material of which it is made causes the ball to return very quickly to its original shape, applying an opposing force to the floor, and pushing the ball upwards. If the floor is soft then it will absorb the energy of the fall, so the ball may bounce very little.

The outcome of this activity becomes difficult to predict due to the varying way in which the floor material absorbs energy, and the elasticity of the ball. Children may be surprised to find that a hard ball will bounce very well on a hard floor, as all the materials are elastic to some degree.

WHAT TO DO

Ask the children some starter questions, such as 'Will the same ball bounce to the same height on different surfaces?', 'Which ball is the bounciest and will it always be the bounciest?', 'What would make a ball bounce poorly?'

Once these questions have been discussed ask the children to plan their investigations, using the 'Investigation planning sheet' (photocopiable page 61). First they need to identify a variable they can change (often called the independent variable) that might affect the way the ball bounces. This is important, as occasionally children start to produce long lists of variables that have little or no relevance to the investigation; for example, the colour of the ball.

Possible independent variables, which might affect the way the ball bounces, could include:
■ the type of ball (the material it is made of)
■ the surface onto which the ball is dropped
■ the height from which the ball is dropped
■ the way the ball is dropped, e.g. let go or thrown.

Once the children have identified some possible independent variables that they could change, they need to identify the variable they could use to measure the effects of the changes (the dependent variable).

Possible dependent variables, which could be used to measure the effects of changes to an independent variable, include:
■ the height to which the ball bounces
■ the number of bounces before the ball comes to rest.

The children now have two lists of variables from which they must choose one to change and one to measure. The remaining possible independent variables are used to describe how the test is made fair – these variables must be kept constant throughout an investigation to ensure that it is a fair test, and that any effects are solely due to the manipulation of the chosen independent variable.

The selection of variables to alter and measure results in the children developing their own questions to investigate. So if the children decide to change the type of ball and measure the height of the bounce, they are investigating questions such as 'When I change the ball, what will happen to the height it bounces?' or 'Which ball will bounce the highest?' At this point the children can make predictions about what they think will happen.

What I have changed: Type of ball	What I have measured: Height of bounce (in cm)			
	Reading 1	Reading 2	Reading 3	Average
sponge ball	20	22	21	21
golf ball	62	61	60	61

The children now need to decide how to carry out their investigation. This involves listing the equipment they will need and describing how they are going use it. They should decide how many measurements they are going to take and at what intervals. They should be aware of how to take repeated readings and calculate an average, and understand in basic terms that this helps to give more representative results by reducing the effects of random variation. The children should record their results in a table, like the one on the previous page.

Here the children have taken repeated measurements and calculated an average. It is usually this average value that they should plot on a graph. Once the children have completed all their measurements they need to produce a graph. The type of graph they produce depends very much on the data they have collected, as summarized in the table below.

Once the graph has been produced, the children can begin to draw conclusions and develop ideas about their investigation. They need to be encouraged to link their conclusions to the development of their scientific knowledge and understanding. The results of the investigation may support an accepted concept and current knowledge and/or demonstrate and introduce a new concept. Some investigations may produce results that are unexpected or even apparently illogical. Here the investigation itself can be used to develop ideas about how such things as the accuracy of measuring can affect results, for example.

In this investigation into bouncing balls of different types, the children need to produce a bar graph. From these results, the children can draw their own conclusions about what they have observed. They should be encouraged to compare their final findings with their original predictions, and comment upon how the investigation has changed or supported their ideas.

DIFFERENTIATION

Investigations of this type provide many opportunities to provide a differentiated activity in science. Less able children may not be able to identify variables to measure, change and keep fair; this can be done for them. If children have difficulty plotting a graph, then the form of some of the data could perhaps be changed from numbers to words, so that they can produce a bar graph instead.

Fair testing is an ideal process for more able children, as they can be set a science problem to investigate by generating their own questions and setting about solving them independently.

What is changed	What is measured	Type of graph
WORDS e.g. type of material	WORDS e.g. does it conduct electricity?	No graph – just a table with descriptions
WORDS e.g. type of surface	NUMBERS e.g. the size of force required to pull a 1kg weight	Bar graph
NUMBERS e.g. number of bulbs	WORDS e.g. brightness of bulb	No graph – just a table with descriptions
WHOLE NUMBERS ONLY e.g. number of elastic bands	NUMBERS e.g. how much an elastic band stretched	Bar graph
NUMBERS e.g. distance of object from screen	NUMBERS e.g. height of shadow	Line graph

NOW OR LATER

Children could be asked to carry out another investigation into the way balls bounce, but this time changing a different independent variable from their original list of 'possibles'. They could use a different dependent variable to measure, too. It may be possible to use the results of their first investigation to predict the outcome of the second.

SOUNDS DREADFUL!

RESOURCES AND CLASSROOM ORGANISATIONS

Each group will need:
■ glass milk bottles
■ water
■ ruler
■ measuring container
■ 'Bottle sounds recording sheet' – photocopiable page 60.

BACKGROUND KNOWLEDGE

Sounds are created when an object vibrates. Actions such as banging, shaking, scraping, plucking strings and blowing through or over holes in pipes cause vibrations in the surrounding air. Sound travels through the air in waves. The size, shape and frequency of these waves determine the volume, quality and pitch of the sound. Sound waves travel through air at a speed of about 344 miles per second.

WHAT TO DO

Ask the children to gently tap a milk bottle without any water in it. Ask them to describe the sound. Ask them to guess what will happen to the sound as they add water. The children should then add 50ml of water to the bottle and then tap it

again. Has the sound changed? How has it changed? Has it got higher or lower in pitch? The children should record their ideas on the 'Bottle sound recording sheet' (photocopiable page 60).

Ask the children to continue to add a little water, and then to test the sound again, until the bottle is full. Ask them to describe what they have observed and to try to explain their observations. How do these observations relate to everyday life, in musical instruments, for example?

In this investigation, the more water there is in the bottle, the higher the pitch of the sound. This is equivalent to shortening the length of a string in a stringed instrument.

SAFETY

Children need to be aware of the risks that accompany any sort of work using objects made of glass.

OBJECTIVES

To develop the following skills:
■ relating observations to scientific knowledge and understanding to explain a range of everyday changes
■ using observations to describe changes.

VOCABULARY

Vibration, sound wave, frequency, wavelength, pitch, amplitude.

NOW OR LATER

■ Children could experiment by changing the water levels in a series of bottles to make musical notes. They could compare the sounds the bottles make with the sounds from a tuned instrument, or set a challenge to play a simple tune using their bottles.

■ A computer could be used to 'see' sounds. Any investigations with sound are enhanced if the children have access to equipment that enables them to 'see' the sound wave and the changes in shape that take place as the sound varies. Such equipment is often outside the budget of a primary school; but a simple sound analyser can be created using any computer running the Windows operating system, since this includes a program called Sound Recorder. With this program running and a simple microphone plugged into the sound card, the children can not only record sounds and play them back, but can also see a simple wave pattern representation of the sound. The children are then able to see how the wave changes shape as the sound changes. This can be achieved to greater effect using a sound sensor and data logging software.

NOT SO DIM!

OBJECTIVES
To develop the following skills:
■ making careful and repeated measurements
■ using specialised measuring equipment
■ using a table and drawing line graphs
■ identifying patterns in line graphs
■ drawing conclusions from the evidence collected.

VOCABULARY
Conductor, insulator, variable resistance, ammeter, electrical energy, graphite, amps.

RESOURCES AND CLASSROOM ORGANIZATION
Each group (or each child, if resources allow) will need:
■ batteries, connectors (e.g. crocodile clips and wires), bulb, bulb holder, ammeter and pencil with 'lead' exposed (to be done by the teacher, using a craft knife), all to be connected in a circuit as shown below
■ ruler
■ 'Data recording sheet' – photocopiable page 62.
An ammeter is a piece of equipment needed to measure electric current. If one is not available, the focus for the investigation could be changed from pattern seeking to observation. The children are able to observe and record the effect on the brightness of a bulb, by changing the length of graphite through which the current has to travel.

BACKGROUND KNOWLEDGE
An electric current is a flow of particles called electrons through a material. Materials such as metal allow the current to flow through them fairly easily. They can be described as conductors of electricity. Materials that do not allow the current to flow easily are described as insulators. Plastics are good electrical insulators. Conductors offer a very low resistance to the flow of particles; insulators offer very high resistance. Some materials, such as graphite (the 'lead' in pencils), are 'in between' – they allow the current to flow, but not very easily. The resistance of a rod of graphite changes according to its length. The greater the resistance, the smaller the electric current that flows.

WHAT TO DO
Carefully split a normal graphite pencil using a craft knife. Mark along the length of the pencil a centimetre scale.

Ask the children to build the circuit shown in the diagram above. Ask them to test the circuit without the pencil to see if it works. Check for faulty components, such as blown bulbs or run down batteries, and change them if necessary.

Explain to the children that it is the graphite in the pencil that they are investigating, not the wood, as that is an insulator and will not conduct electricity. This can be demonstrated by connecting the wires to the wood of the pencil, rather than to the graphite – the bulb will not light up.

Discuss with the children what is happening in a simple circuit. They will need to be aware that current flows around a circuit and that it is this flow of energy that makes the bulb light up.

We can measure that flow of energy using an ammeter. Record the level of current without the pencil in the circuit, so that the connecting wires are in direct contact. Ask the children to predict what will happen when they then connect the pencil in the circuit with the crocodile clips less than a centimetre apart on the graphite.

Now the children should start the investigation, connecting the crocodile clips at every centimetre mark along the graphite, and recording the readings shown on the ammeter. As problems may occur in obtaining a good contact with the graphite, the children should take at least three readings at each mark to improve accuracy.

Readings can be recorded in the table on the 'Data recording sheet' (photocopiable page 62) and the average electric current for each mark calculated. The children can then use these readings to plot a line graph, with the length of graphite in centimetres along the (horizontal) x-axis and the electric current in amps along the (vertical) y-axis. The children should observe a downward trend on the graph, showing that as the length of graphite increases, the size of the electric current decreases, because the resistance through which it must travel increases. The children need to offer their own ideas about what is happening in the circuit. Encourage them to try to visualize how the electric current is flowing around the circuit.

Discuss with the children their results and findings, and how 'variable resistors' based on this principle are used in everyday life, such as in volume controls and light dimmers.

DIFFERENTIATION

More able children could investigate other non-metallic conductors, such as salt water, and record the changes in current as they change the amount of salt in the solution.

Less able children could test a number of materials in place of the graphite in the circuit and use the readings on the ammeter to sort them into conductors and insulators.

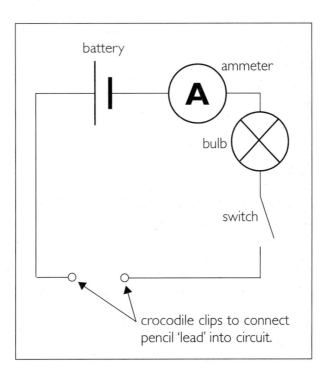

SAFETY

Remind the children that they should always use caution when dealing with electricity, and that mains electricity is extremely dangerous.

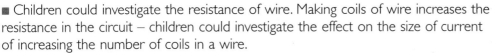
crocodile clips to connect pencil 'lead' into circuit.

NOW OR LATER

■ Children could investigate the resistance of wire. Making coils of wire increases the resistance in the circuit – children could investigate the effect on the size of current of increasing the number of coils in a wire.
■ Children could use the pencil variable resistor to control the speed of a small electric motor. They could then incorporate the circuit into a model of a fairground ride or buggy.

Planet information

Planet	Distance from Sun x150million km	Orbit time x Earth years	Mass x Earth's mass	Diameter km	Comp-osition	Moons	Rings	Length of day Earth time
Mercury	58	0.24	0.055	4960	solid	0	0	59 days
Venus	108	0.62	0.814	12003	solid	0	0	243 days
Earth	150	1.00	1.00	12800	solid	1	0	24 hours
Mars	228	1.88	0.107	6720	solid	2	0	24.6 hours
Jupiter	780	11.86	318	140800	gas	16	0	9.8 hours
Saturn	1430	29.46	95.2	113600	gas	18	7	10.2 hours
Uranus	2877	84.01	14.5	51200	gas	15	11	15.5 hours
Neptune	4509	164.79	17.1	49600	gas	8	4	15.8 hours
Pluto	5928	247.70	0.00216	3200	solid	1	0	6.4 days

Use the table below to make a scale model of the solar system

These are only approximate measurements

Planet	Diameter (cm)	Distance (from sun, cm)	Object
Sun	230	0	2m diameter paper circle
Mercury	0.8	83	small purple bead
Venus	2	155	regular yellow marble
Earth	2	215	regular blue and white marble
Mars	1	326	1cm red bead
Jupiter	23	1,111	white football, decorated
Saturn	19	2,083	foam ball with paper rings
Uranus	8.5	3,009	greenish tennis ball
Neptune	8	6,481	blue racquet ball
Pluto	0.4	8,333	ballbearing

Make a helicopter

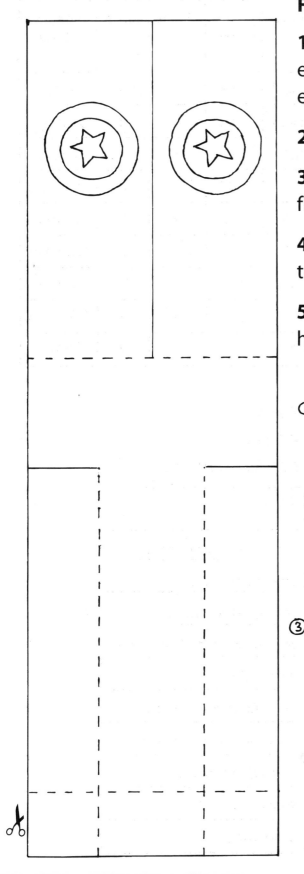

First, cut out the template.

1 Hold the template with the short edge away from you, and cut a slot at each side.

2 Fold in the flaps on each side.

3 Tuck up the bottom of the folded flap, and hold it with a paper clip.

4 Cut along the vertical line at the top to create two 'wings'.

5 Fold out the wings, drop the helicopter, and watch it spin!

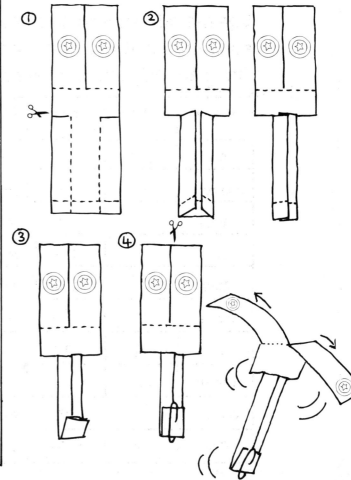

Bottle sounds recording sheet

How did the bottle sound without water?

What do you think will happen to the sound when water is added?

Amount of water (in ml)	What happened to the sound

Describe how we use this discovery:

Name _____   Date _____

Investigation planning sheet

Things I could change:

Things I could measure:

My question:

My prediction:

I will need this equipment:

This is what I will do in the next investigation:

Name   Date

Data recording sheet

My question:

What I have changed:	What I have measured:		
	Reading 1	Reading 2	Reading 3	Average

To calculate an average value, add reading 1, reading 2 and reading 3 together and divide by 3. This will be your final reading.

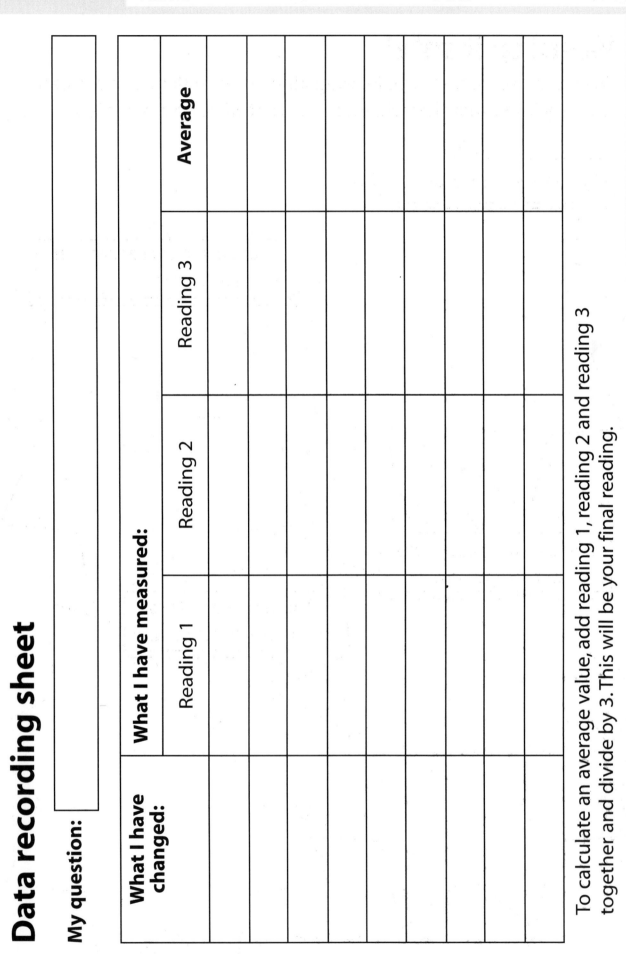

Name   Date

Keeping it safe!

Whenever we do a science investigation we must think about safety. It is very important that whatever we work with, we work safely.

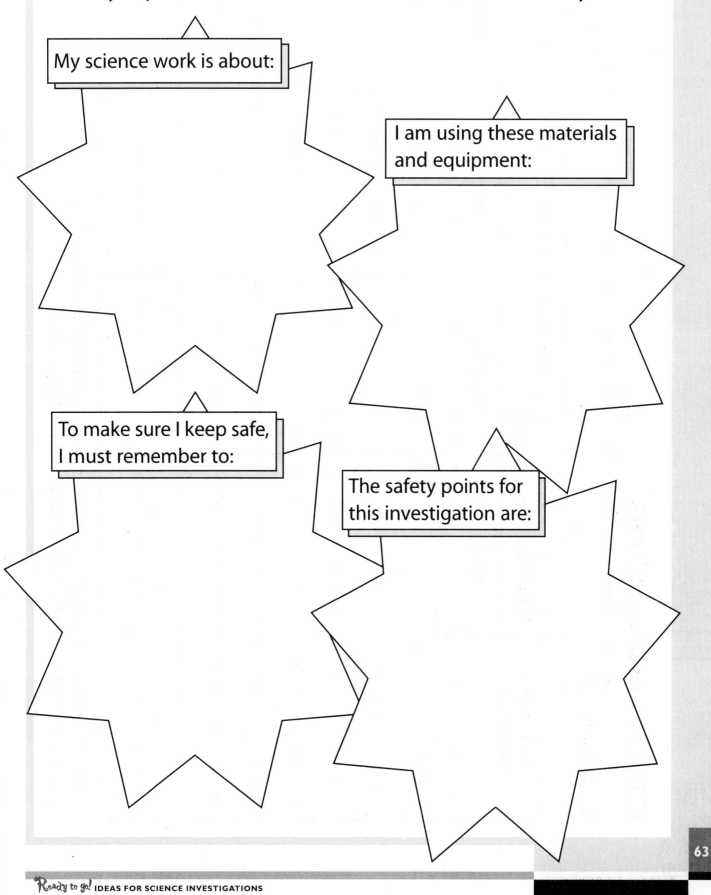

My science work is about:

I am using these materials and equipment:

To make sure I keep safe, I must remember to:

The safety points for this investigation are:

Ready to go! **IDEAS FOR SCIENCE INVESTIGATIONS**

ACTIVITIES																						SKILLS: Children have opportunities to…	
NOT SO DIM!	SOUNDS DREADFUL!	BALLS AND BOUNCING	STRETCHING	ME AND MY SHADOW	HELICOPTERS	HOW OLD WOULD I BE ON VENUS?	PUSH-PULL-O-METER	SILLY MIXTURE	DRYING THE WASHING	AMAZING RAISINS	PHLUBBER!!	ONE OR TWO SUGARS?	KNEE BONE IS CONNECTED TO THE LEG BONE!	WHERE WOULD YOU FIND THE MOST DAISIES?	WHEN I GROW UP I WANT TO BE A HEALTHY PLANT!	BRUSHING YOUR TEETH	DO PLANTS LIKE LEMONADE?	ROTTEN TOWERS	DESIGN-A-GENES	BEETLE ALLSORTS	BEAT THE CLOCK	Skill	Category
✓	✓	✓	✓	✓	✓	✓	✓	✓	✓	✓	✓	✓	✓	✓	✓	✓	✓	✓	✓	✓	✓	Apply ideas and knowledge and understanding of science to the world around them	The Nature of Science
✓	✓	✓	✓	✓	✓		✓	✓	✓	✓	✓	✓	✓	✓	✓	✓	✓	✓	✓	✓	✓	Consider information obtained from their own work and other sources	
✓	✓	✓	✓	✓	✓	✓	✓	✓	✓	✓	✓	✓	✓	✓	✓	✓	✓	✓	✓	✓	✓	Understand that scientific ideas can be tested through observation and measurement	
✓	✓	✓	✓	✓	✓	✓	✓	✓	✓	✓	✓	✓	✓	✓	✓	✓	✓	✓	✓	✓	✓	Report their work in speech and writing using the relevant scientific vocabulary	Communicating in Science
✓	✓	✓	✓	✓	✓	✓	✓	✓	✓	✓	✓	✓	✓	✓	✓	✓	✓	✓	✓	✓	✓	Use a range of methods to record and present information	
✓	✓	✓	✓	✓	✓	✓	✓	✓	✓	✓	✓	✓	✓	✓	✓	✓	✓	✓	✓	✓	✓	Use ICT to present information	
✓	✓	✓	✓	✓				✓													✓	Use standard measures and SI units	
✓	✓	✓	✓	✓	✓		✓		✓		✓		✓		✓		✓	✓				Turn ideas suggested to them, and their own ideas, into a form that can be investigated	Investigative Skills
			✓	✓	✓	✓			✓		✓	✓	✓		✓	✓					✓	Ask questions and use their knowledge and understanding of the context when planning an investigation to consider what may happen	
			✓	✓	✓	✓	✓		✓	✓		✓	✓		✓	✓	✓	✓	✓			Decide what information should be collected	
			✓	✓	✓	✓			✓		✓		✓		✓	✓					✓	Understand that in situations where factors can be identified and controlled, a fair test may be carried out	
✓		✓	✓		✓		✓	✓		✓	✓		✓	✓		✓	✓	✓		✓	✓	Consider what resources to use	
✓	✓	✓	✓	✓	✓		✓	✓	✓	✓	✓		✓	✓		✓					✓	Recognize and assess the hazards and risks to themselves and others	
✓	✓	✓	✓	✓	✓		✓	✓	✓	✓	✓		✓	✓	✓	✓	✓				✓	Use resources correctly, taking action to control risks	
✓	✓	✓	✓	✓	✓	✓	✓	✓	✓	✓	✓	✓	✓	✓	✓	✓	✓	✓	✓		✓	Make careful observations and measurements and record them appropriately	
✓		✓		✓	✓		✓							✓			✓				✓	Check observations and measurements by repeating them, when this is appropriate.	
	✓		✓		✓							✓				✓			✓			Use ICT equipment and software to monitor changes	
✓		✓	✓	✓	✓	✓		✓		✓	✓	✓	✓	✓		✓	✓		✓		✓	Make comparisons and identify and describe trends in data	
✓	✓	✓	✓	✓	✓	✓		✓	✓	✓		✓	✓	✓	✓	✓	✓	✓	✓	✓	✓	Use results of their investigations to draw conclusions	
✓	✓	✓	✓	✓	✓	✓		✓	✓		✓	✓	✓	✓	✓	✓		✓	✓	✓	✓	Relate the outcomes of their investigation or their conclusions to their scientific knowledge and understanding	
	✓				✓		✓		✓	✓			✓		✓	✓		✓	✓	✓	✓	Review their work and suggest how data could be improved	
			3E		6F	6E	5E	4E	4D	5C	6D	3C	6C	6A		3B	3A	5B	6B	5B	4B / 5A	QCA Ref. Unit	
			Sc4, 2d	Sc4, 3a, 3b, 3d	Sc4, 2b, 2c, 2d, 2f, 2g, 2h	Sc4, 4d	Sc4, 2b, 2c, 2d, 2f, 2g	Sc4, 2b, 2c, 2d, 2f, 2g	Sc3, 3b, 3c	Sc3, 2c, 2d, 2e	Sc3, 3a, 2c	Sc3, 1a, 1e	Sc3, 2a, 2c	Sc2, 5a, 5b	Sc2, 1b, 3a, 3c	Sc2, 2a	Sc2, 1b, 3a, 3c	Sc2, 5e	Sc2, 1a, 2g	Sc2, 4a	Sc2, 2c, 2d, 2e	National Curriculum References	